G000016029

OPEN-SEZ-ME

FOREWORD

'WHAT SHALL WE DO WITH THE CHILDREN TODAY?'

If you are a carer of young children, you've probably asked this question a thousand times!

After working with children for over twenty years, I found thinking up new ideas to be an endless struggle. This prompted me to research the material for Open-Sez-Me, the series of books that I had always wanted.

OPEN-SEZ-ME SUMMER is the third book in a series of four, which are set in each of the seasons. This unique collection of books opens the door to a wealth of information, ideas and activities from many different cultures, providing enjoyable learning and lots of fun! - all year round. Every volume is designed to help children to observe and experience the world around them.

The aim is thus to provide a useful resource book for the carers of young children aged two to seven. In addition, older children may find it a helpful guide to seasonal projects.

Shirley West

CONTENTS

JUNE

JULY

COOKING PAGE

STORIES AND SONGS

POEMS

AUGUST

FACTS   PAGE

THINGS TO DO

STORIES AND SONGS   PAGE

POEMS

COOKING

STORIES AND SONGS

POEMS

JUNE

'June brings tulips, lilies, roses
Fills the childrens' hands with posies'

Summer begins at the summer solstice. This is the longest day - and the shortest night-of the year, normally around the 21st of June. Summer ends at the Autumn equinox. This usually occurs on 22nd September and is one of the two occasions in the year when day and night are of equal length. The summer solstice in the southern hemisphere is the 22nd December.

WHAT DOES SUMMER BRING?

A story to read

June is the noisiest month of the year and the earth is full of scurrying activity. Look inside nooks and crannies and see what you can find.

First you might find lots of ants living in their miniature cities which are full of tiny passageways. Ants can be seen scurrying about doing their daily chores. They heap twigs, dead leaves and pine needles at their entrance which stops the rain from getting in.

A long line of worker ants leaves the nest in search of food. One of them finds a beetle but it's too big for just one ant to manage, so all the ants get together and drag the beetle home. Other ants keep busy underground: some build and clean the nest; some stand by the entrance to guard it; some look after the eggs.

Dragonflies, with their brightly coloured wings, are found by ponds and rivers. They can fly very fast. The dragonfly has a huge appetite and in half an hour it can eat its own weight.

The house fly has pads of tiny hairs on its feet and this is why it can cling to anything, walking on ceilings or up walls. The female will lay hundreds of eggs which hatch into maggots.

The sunny sky is filled with birds, bees butterflies and moths. The days are longer and there is more time for everyone to play!

ALL ABOUT BEES

THE LIFE OF A BEE

A story to read

Many bees are kept in hives. Wild bees and bumblebees make nests in holes in the ground or in trees. There are three types of bees. They are the workers, the drones, and the queen.

There are thousands of workers in one hive. These are all female and they have stings. Each worker has a different duty. There are ones to gather pollen, which is used for feeding the bees. There are varnishers, who seal the cells and fill in any cracks in the hive. Then there are workers that act as chemists - they put a little formic acid into each honey-cell before it is sealed. While all this is going on some workers will guard against intruders, some will remove all the rubbish, some will be the water carriers and others will flap their wings like a fan to keep the hive cool.

The drones are the male bees. They don't have stings and they do no work. The drones' only job is to mate with the queen bee.

The queen bee lays hundreds of tiny white eggs. She lays each one in a tiny cell. After three days a little white grub called a larva hatches and the nursing bee feeds it with honey and a special food called bee milk.

By the eighth day the larvae are almost fully grown. The worker bees then cover the top of each cell with wax.

Three weeks after the eggs were laid, the bee is fully grown. It chews its way out of the cell but it cannot fly yet.

The young bee is fed on honey and pollen. This is collected by the honey bee who flits from flower to flower gathering pollen in her leg-baskets. When she gets home she scrapes it off and makes bee-bread to feed the young.

The larvae that will become queen bees are reared in larger cells. They are fed on lots of creamy food called Royal Jelly. The queen bees take only sixteen days to develop. After a few days they leaves the hive to find mates.

When autumn comes, the old queen bee, the workers and the drones all die. But the new queen bees live until the next year. Then in spring the whole cycle starts again.

BUSY BEES

Busy, busy, busy,
Buzzing, buzzing, buzzing,
Went the busy, buzzing bees.

Fly, fly, flying,
Flap, flap, flapping,
Flew the flying, flapping,
Busy, buzzing, bees.

Hum, hum, humming,
Drum, drum, drumming,
Zoomed the humming, drumming,
Flying, flapping,
Busy, buzzing, bees.

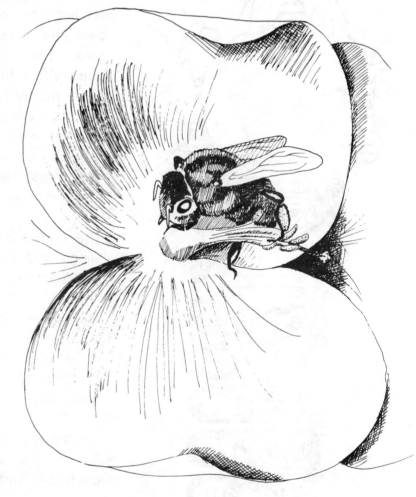

Suggested songs: **Zum! Zum! Zum!**, from **Infant Joy a Complete Repertoire of Songs,** published by University of London Press.

THINGS TO DO

A HONEYCOMB

YOU WILL NEED

16 egg boxes, yellow paint for the honey-comb, shearing elastic, bakers clay (page 18)

METHOD

1. Cut each of the six sections out of all the egg boxes and staple them together to form any shape. Paint the honeycomb yellow.

2. Form the bakers clay into little oval shapes for the bees. Make a small hole in the middle of the bee with a needle, and bake for 1 hour 150 'C/300 'F/Gas 2.

3. Paint the bees and allow to dry. Thread some of the bees with 25 cm (10") of shearing elastic, and hang them with sello-tape from the honey comb. Place the other bees inside the egg box.

Make a frieze depicting a beehive and the honey comb, and bees flying around using the method above.

TALK ABOUT WHAT BEES PRODUCE

Honey is used in sandwiches, cakes, biscuits, sweets and mead.

Beeswax is used in furniture and floor polish, cough medicine, cold-creams, and for clean-ing the face.

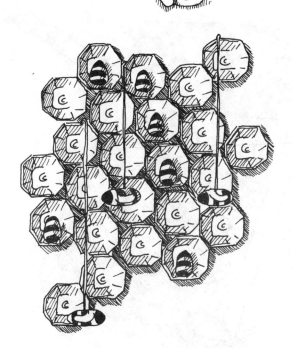

COOKING

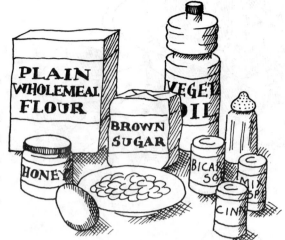

'What do you like doing best in the world, Pooh?'

'Well,' said Pooh, 'what I like best....' and then he had to stop and think. Because although Eating Honey was a very good thing to do, there was a moment just before you began to eat it which was better that when you were, but he didn't know what it was called.'

From The House at Pooh Corner by A. A. Milne.

HONEY NUT SQUARES

YOU WILL NEED

110 g (4 oz) plain wholemeal flour
50 g (2 oz) flaked almonds
50 g (2 oz) brown sugar
110 g (4 oz) honey
1 teaspoon of bicarbonate of soda
2 teaspoons of vegetable oil
1 teaspoon of mixed spices
1 teaspoon of cinnamon
1 large egg
pinch of salt

Oven temperature: 190' C/375' F/ Gas 5

METHOD

1. Sift together the flour, bicarbonate soda, spices and salt.

2. Add the sugar and honey. Beat the egg and oil together and stir into the mixture (if too dry, add a little milk).

3. Grease a small square baking tin and pour the mixture into it. Smooth the top and sprinkle with the nuts. Bake for 20-25 minutes, and cut into squares when cool.

FLOWER FESTIVAL

Any time from June to August

In Tissington in Derbyshire you might come across a 10 foot tall coloured picture near a spring or tap. This is made up from natural objects such as pebbles, flower petals, leaves, moss, wild fruit and small stones. This form of picture making is called **Well-Dressing**. Its history goes back to pagan times, when the people believed in water-nymphs, who had to be kept happy so that they would allow the water to continue flowing.

Tissington Water, flowing clear and cold from the limestone springs, is believed to have saved the village from the terrible **'Black Death'** plague (1349) which struck so many neighbouring Derbyshire towns.

Nowadays, Well-Dressing is the giving of thanks to God for the gift of water, and usually illustrates stories from the Bible.

In Tissington this festival is held on **May 9th**, Ascension Day. But in other parts of England it may be held right up to August.

Suggested Songs, **I Like The Flowers**, from **Flying Around**, published by A.C. Black.

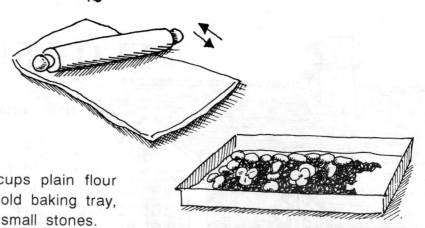

THINGS TO DO

WELL-DRESSING

YOU WILL NEED

4 tablespoons cooking oil, 4 cups plain flour
2 cups salt, 2 cups water, an old baking tray,
moss, pebbles, petals, leaves, small stones.

METHOD

Mix all the ingredients together, then roll out
the dough until it is 2cm thick. Place it in a
large baking tray and cover it with petals,
pebbles, leaves and moss. Put in a warm place
and allow to dry over a period of 3-4 days.

WALL FLOWER PLAQUE

YOU WILL NEED

Bakers Clay

4 cups plain flour, 1 cup salt, 1and 1/2 cups
water, poster paints, varnish, string.

Oven temperature: 150 'C/300 'F/Gas 2

METHOD

1. Mix all the ingredients together. Knead
until firm as you would dough. Place some of
dough in a small baking tray and make a hole
in the middle about 2cm from the top.

2. With the rest of the dough, cut out flowers
with stalks and leaves. Cut out small thin
strips for the grass. Wet the dough a little
and place the flower in the middle of the tray
and the grass at the bottom.

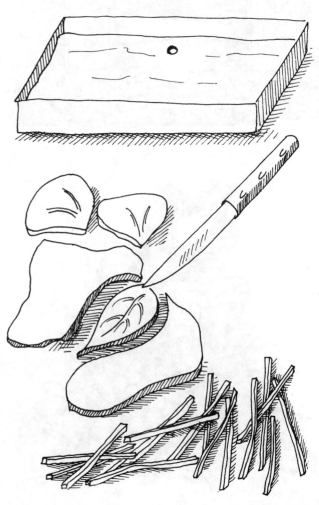

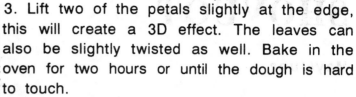

3. Lift two of the petals slightly at the edge, this will create a 3D effect. The leaves can also be slightly twisted as well. Bake in the oven for two hours or until the dough is hard to touch.

4. When the plaque has cooled, paint and then varnish. Once dry, thread the string through the hole and hang on a wall.

COOKING

ELDER FLOWER DRINK

<u>METHOD</u>

The cluster of white flowers can be made into a drink by pouring boiling water on them. Then allow to cool before straining.

MARIGOLD EGGS

The marigold's bright petals can be used as a herb and as a colourant. Fresh or dried, it is good in puddings, cakes, salads, and meat dishes. It colours rice, noodles and soups.

To dry the petals spread them on a baking tray or foil and cook in a very slow oven for two hours or until they are dry enough to crumble. Store them in airtight jars.

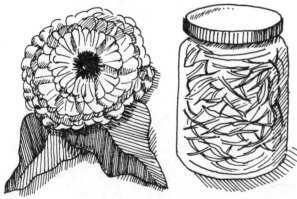

<u>YOU WILL NEED</u>

Hard boiled eggs, marigolds, mayonnaise.

<u>METHOD</u>

1. Slice the eggs in half lengthwise. Take out the yolks and mash them together with some mayonnaise, dried and crushed marigold petals, and season. Refill the egg whites with the mixture. Take fresh marigold petals and tuck them into the centres of the stuffed eggs until each egg is a flower.

SHOVUOT

May/June

Shovuot, the Jewish festival of weeks, comes seven weeks or fifty days after the Passover. The festival celebrates the harvest season in Israel. The first fruits of the harvest are offered to God in the Synagogue. Shovuot also commemorates the anniversary of the giving of the ten commandments at Mount Sinai.

During the 19th century, the festival was recognized as the day of confirmation, when young people of thirteen years of age were confirmed in the faith at a special ceremony. Previously, only boys were permitted to go through this ceremony known as Bar Mitzvah, but now both boys and girls are confirmed when they are thirteen.

This summer festival is commemorated today by decorating the house and Synagogue with seasonal plants and flowers.

A special service is held and the Bible story of Ruth is often read. It is about a non-Jewish girl who was the ancestor of the Jewish King David.

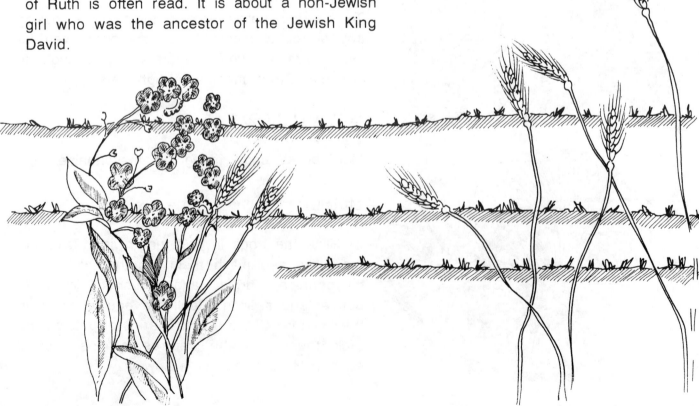

THE STORY OF RUTH

A story to read

This story begins in Bethlehem, in a time of hardship and very little food.

A farmer named Elimelech with his wife, Naomi, and their two sons, decided to move to Moab, in order to find better fortune. Sadly Elimelech died, and life was very hard for Naomi and her sons.

But soon the boys grew up and married. The oldest son married a girl called Ruth. They all lived happily for ten years until one day both the two sons were killed in an accident.

Naomi was very sad and lonely without her sons. So she decided to go back to Bethlehem. Ruth asked to go with her saying:

> 'Wherever you go, I will go
> Wherever you live, I will live.
> Your people shall be my people
> and your God, my God'.

Back in Bethlehem things were much better than before. But Naomi and Ruth found it very difficult to find food.

One day Ruth went into the fields to collect the corn that the farmer had left. The owner of the field, Boaz, saw Ruth, fell in love with her, and married her. And Naomi and Ruth were never hungry again.

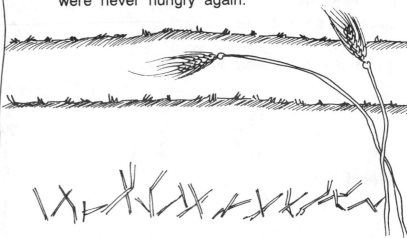

THINGS TO DO

FLOWERS IN A VASE

YOU WILL NEED

FOR THE FLOWERS

Paper, paints, tissue paper.

FOR THE VASE

2 tablespoons cooking oil, 2 cups plain flour, 1 cup of salt, 1 cup of water, half a washing up liquid bottle, flower petals.

METHOD

1. Cut out two sizes of petals one 12 cm (5") and 18 cm (7") in diameter as shown. Paint either side and allow to dry. Glue small balls of torn tissue paper onto the petals.

2. For the stem roll a sheet of A4 lengthways, as tight as possible, and paint green.

3. Glue the smaller petal to the larger one in the middle. Staple the stem to the back of the petals.

4. For the vase, mix the cooking oil, flour, salt, and water together to make a dough. Roll the dough out. Mould it to the outside of the washing up bottle as shown. Press on the flower petals and allow to dry in a warm place for several days.

5. Arrange the flowers in the vase.

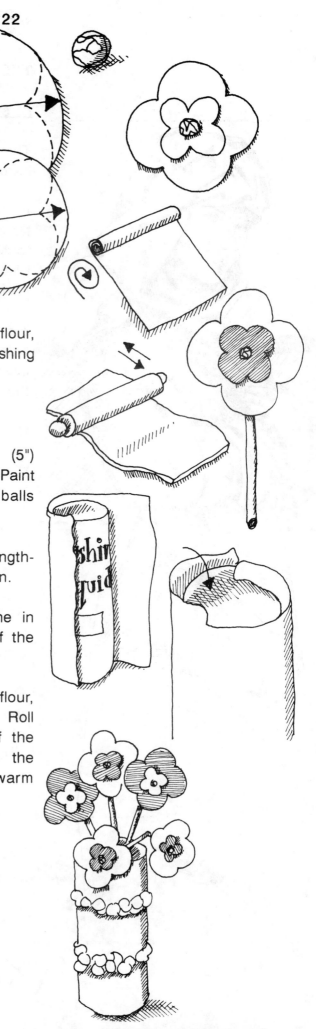

COOKING

Milk, cheese and honey are the symbolic foods of Shavuot.

CHEESE CAKE

<u>YOU WILL NEED</u>

350 g (12 oz) curd or cottage cheese, sieved
175 g (6 oz) digestive biscuits
425 ml (1/2 pt) sour cream
75 g (3 oz) sugar
75 g (3 oz) butter
2 eggs, beaten
vanilla essence

Oven temperature: 180 'C/350 'F/Gas 4

<u>METHOD</u>

1. Butter a 23 cm (9") ovenproof flan dish.

2. Crush the biscuits with a rolling pin and mix with 25 g (1 oz) of sugar. Melt the butter and add to the mixture. Press the crumb mixture to the sides and base of the flan dish.

3. Bake in the centre of the oven for 10 minutes.

4. Meanwhile, beat the cheese until soft and mix in the eggs, then add the rest of the sugar and the sour cream. Add a little vanilla essence and pour into the biscuit crust. Return the cake to the oven and bake for 30-35 minutes, until set.

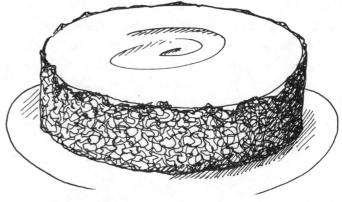

BAGELS

You take a hole, and you put some dough around it!

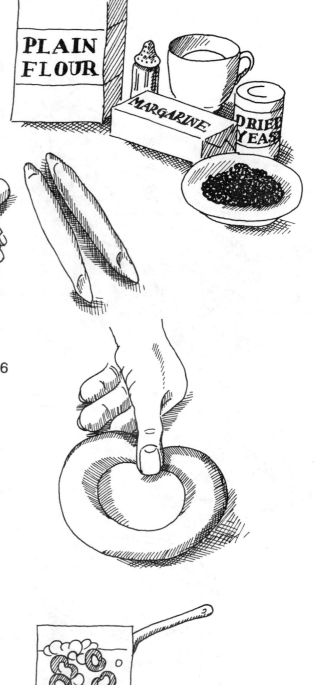

YOU WILL NEED

225 g (8 oz) plain flour
50 g (2 oz) margarine
1 cup milk, scalded
2 tablespoons dried yeast
water
salt
sesame, poppy, or caraway seeds

Oven temperature: pre-heat 200' C/400' F/Gas 6

METHOD

1. Melt the margarine in the scalded milk. Proof the yeast with a pinch of sugar in the warm water as instructed on the packet.

2. Combine the two liquid mixtures and gradually blend in the flour and salt until a soft, sticky dough is formed. Knead well. Cover and leave it to double in size.

3. Boil 425 ml (3/4 pt) water with 2 teaspoons of salt.

4. Knead dough again on a floured board. Break off each piece about the size of a plum and roll out into a 12 cm (5") long snake-like shape, tapering the dough at its ends. Twist into a circle and press the ends together.

5. Allow to stand for 10 minutes. Drop the bagels one by one into the boiling water, boiling a few at a time. Cover and wait until the water boils again. Turn the bagels, cover again, and wait until the water boils for 2 minutes. Remove and place on a greased baking tray. Sprinkle with caraway seeds and bake for 30 minutes until golden brown.

WESAK

May/June

Wesak or Vesakha is one of the most important festivals in the Buddhist calendar and takes place on, or near to, the May full moon.

The festival celebrates the three most important events in the life of Buddha: his birth and death day, and the moment when he learnt the truth about life and how to avoid suffering.

The celebrations last for three days. Houses and shrines are decorated with flowers, candles and lanterns. Special offerings are made to statues of the Buddha and there are processions in the streets.

A DAY IN THE LIFE OF A YOUNG BUDDHIST

A story to read

Gotama is a monk and he is only nine years old. His day starts at five o'clock in the morning with a drink and reading a book about the teachings of Buddha.

He washes in the open air with cold water before attending the morning service, after which he can finally have his breakfast.

Dressed in orange clothes, he goes off with his friends in single file to the local villages to collect food. In return for the food they offer prayers to the villagers.

When Gotama gets back he offers the food to the Lord Buddha, then the food is shared amongst everyone.

After the evening meal Gotama reads once again the teachings of Buddha till late in the evening. He has to read out aloud all the time so that the priest can hear him.

As the evening falls, the bell is rung and the Abbot leads the young monks in their final meditation. As they sit crossed-legged and with their eyes closed, he asks them to remember the words of Buddha:

'I have revealed to you as many things as there are leaves in a great tree. But as many things have been revealed to me as there are leaves in a forest.'

With this prayer Gotama's day has ended and he is ready for sleep.

THE LIFE OF BUDDHA

Buddha was the son of a King in Northern India called Sakya. His mother was called Queen Mahamaya. She had a baby and named him Siddharta, which means **wish fulfilled**. His mother died when he was only seven years old.

When he grew up, Siddharta married, and had a son. But one day he decided to leave the life of a prince and rode off on his horse Kanthaka until he came to the river Anoma. There he cut off his long hair with his sword and changed his royal clothing for the orange robe of a beggar. He changed his name to Gautam and lived in an Ashram which is a place of meditation.

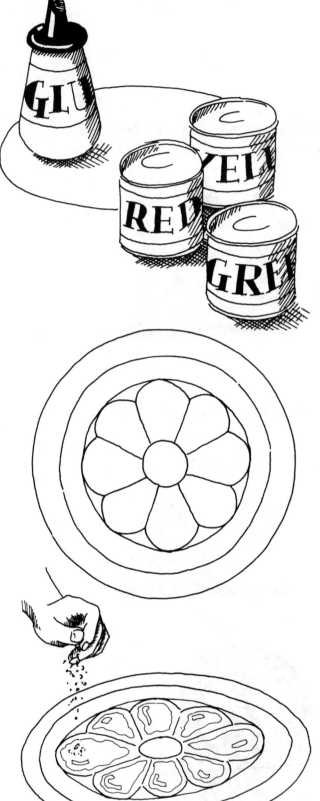

In order to learn about suffering he hardly ate. In the summer he would stay out in the burning sun, and in winter he bathed in icy water. At the age of thirty-five he became enlightened as the full moon of Vesakha (May) was setting. He became known as **The Fully Enlightened One** or **Buddha** and taught his beliefs for over forty years.

The Buddha's teaching was not concerned with God but with how people can live in harmony. He said that human wants and desires were the basis of all suffering. If people gave up their desires they would no longer suffer.

THINGS TO DO

Tibetans and Nepalese use bright colours in their painting because they believe colours symbolize different parts of the mind. A circle known as a **mandala** is used as an aid for concentration. This helps the mind to reach enlightenment.

MAKE A MANDALA

YOU WILL NEED

Large round sheet of white paper, bright powder paints, glue.

METHOD

1. Draw the circles on the sheet of paper as shown.

2. Glue the inner circles and sprinkle each one with a different coloured powder paint.

Suggested Songs: **Sinhales Lullaby**, from **A Musical Calendar of Festivals**, published by Ward Lock Educational.

HAND GESTURES IN BUDDHIST ART

Teach the children these gestures of the hands and fingers. In Buddhist art these have special meanings, and are called **mudras**.

Turning the Wheel of the Law

One hand is raised in a gesture of protection, while the other hand grants a wish.

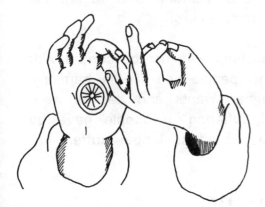

The hands are 'calling the earth to witness'. When Buddha became enlightened he touched the earth.

This is the gesture of teaching

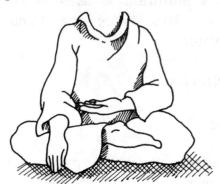

THE GOLDEN BUDDHA

A large golden Buddha
In a golden temple stands
With a tiny lotus flower
Held in his golden hand.
His eyes are full of wisdom,
There's a smile upon his face.
He teaches people about freedom,
And of his love for the human race.

By Shirley West

COOKING

EIGHT TREASURE RICE (Babao Fan)

Traditionally this is served at any festive occasion. This rice must contain eight treasures or charms to banish evil spirits away. When the eight treasures are considered to represent the eight lotus petals of Buddhism, the recipe will include lotus seeds. In this case, the dish is known as Ba Bao ('lotus seed') Fan. The treasures may include sweet beans, dates, almonds, peanuts, melon seeds, raisins, dried apricots, walnuts.

YOU WILL NEED

2 cups rice
2 tablespoons margarine
3 tablespoons brown sugar
any dried fruits and nuts

METHOD

1. Wash the rice and boil until tender. Drain and stir in the margarine and sugar.

2. Grease the bottom and sides of a pudding basin and arrange alternate layers of cooked rice with fruit and nuts. Press the fruit and nuts so that the colours will show when the dish is turned out.

3. Cover with foil and steam the pudding for 40 minutes. Turn out on to a serving dish and decorate with nuts.

VEGETABLE PARATHA

All Buddhists are vegetarian.

YOU WILL NEED

450 g (1 lb) plain wholemeal flour
120-175 mls (4-6 fl oz) water
melted margarine
grated raw cauliflower
pinch of salt

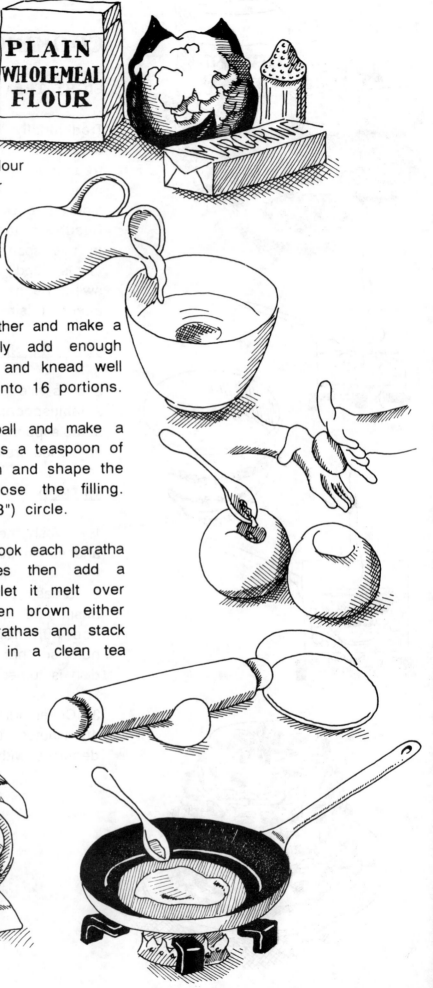

METHOD

1. Mix the flour and salt together and make a well in the centre. Gradually add enough water to make a soft dough and knead well until no longer sticky. Divide into 16 portions.

2. Roll each portion into a ball and make a depression in the middle. Press a teaspoon of cauliflower into the depression and shape the dough into a ball to enclose the filling. Carefully roll out into 8 cm (3") circle.

3. Gently heat a frying pan. Cook each paratha on each side for 2 minutes then add a teaspoon of margarine and let it melt over the surface. Turn until golden brown either side. Cook the remaining parathas and stack them on top of each other in a clean tea towel.

ENVIRONMENTAL DAY

June 5th

The United Nations Conference on the Human Environment, held at Stockholm in June 1972, proclaimed the right of human beings to live in a healthy environment. They undertook the responsibility to protect and improve that environment for future generations.

UNDERSTANDING THE ENVIRONMENT

Water, oxygen and other elements are vital for the continuation of life. This is why many of nature's processes work in cycles. There is a constant exchange of the elements between air, earth, water, plants and animals, and the recycling processes ensure that all living things are able to live and grow.

When we start to interfere with the law of nature, the cycle of nature is broken. Over the past few years the world has become more aware of environment problems, and it is up to us to teach the next generations.

Fast foods started in America, just over thirty years ago. The trouble was, and is, that the land used to graze the cattle was not really suitable. So large areas of the rainforest were chopped down to provide grazing land for the cattle. With these trees gone, the soil soon lost its nutrients, and after a few years, it becomes useless for grazing cattle, so more trees are chopped down.

Britain and Europe breed their own cattle for burgers, but there is still a problem because these cattle are fed on food that makes them grow quickly, such as soys beans. Soya beans are grown mostly in Brazil, and enormous forests have been cleared to make fields for growing soya.

THINGS TO DO

RECYCLING WASTE

Unlike nature, we are guilty of producing vast amounts of waste.

Talk to the children about rubbish that is thrown away and decide what can be recycled.

Aluminium cans - these can be washed and crushed (stand on them) and taken to a can recycling centre. Only aluminium cans can be recycled - these are not magnetic.

Glass - most places have bottle banks for any kind of glass.

Plastic - cannot be recycled but plastic shopping bags can always be re-used.

WHAT IS ORGANIC WASTE?

This is anything that will rot. To find out what is organic try the following experiment.

YOU WILL NEED

6 12 cm (5") flower pots, a piece of paper, some wool, a plastic cup, aluminium foil, bread, an apple core, earth, water, tray, labels.

METHOD

1. Bury each of the above items in a separate pot and label them.

2. Water every day. After 30 days tip each pot into a tray and note what has happened to each of the items. If they have disintegrated this means they are bio-degradable. This means that natural organisms can break them up.

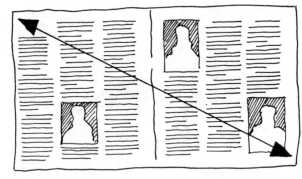

NEWSPAPER SANDALS

It takes 4,000 trees every day to produce just one daily paper. Here is one way to recycle paper.

<u>YOU WILL NEED</u>

8-9 large sheets of newspaper, cardboard, sellotape, PVA glue.

<u>METHOD</u>

1. Diagonally roll each sheet of paper tightly to make long strips. Flatten and tape down. Make one strip smaller than the others.

2. Snake each roll of paper round each other. Tape each end down as you go along, always remembering to start where you left off.

3. To form the band across the shoe place the smaller band into the second outer circle as shown.

4. Cut out a piece of cardboard to fit inside the sandal and glue securely.

DON'T THROW IT AWAY

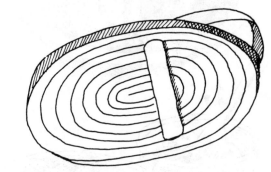

Recycling waste is a very good thing,
A cleaner world it will bring.
If you can use it don't throw it away,
Recycle your waste every day.

But if you do have any rubbish,
A piece of paper or an apple core.
Make sure you put it in the bin,
And not down on the floor!

By Shirley West

COOKING

Buy food that is grown organically. Food that has been treated with pesticides has had a devastating effect on wildlife. Pesticides not only kill off pests, they also poison animals which are harmless. Not only that, think about the cost to the environment and our health!

NUT BURGERS

YOU WILL NEED

110 g (4 oz) ground nuts
110 g (4 oz) wholemeal breadcrumbs
seasoning to taste
a little milk

METHOD

1. Mix the nuts, breadcrumbs and seasoning together.

2. Mix in just enough milk for the mixture to stick together. Form into burger shapes. Lightly fry for a minute on each side.

BUBBLE AND SQUEAK

YOU WILL NEED

left over mashed potato
left over brussel sprouts
any meat or fish left over
flour   oil for frying

METHOD

1. Mash the potato and brussel sprouts together with a fork.

2. Dice the meat or fish and stir into the mixture. Make small flat balls and roll in the flour. Then fry gently until crispy and brown.

DRAGON BOAT FESTIVAL

June 5th

Carved dragon boats take part in a traditional race off the coast of Hong Kong. The race is held during an ancient festival to remember a Chinese poet called Ch'u Yüen who lived over 2000 years ago. Nowadays the race is international, and in 1990 for the first time, there were separate events for men and women.

In some parts, the festival is also known as Poet's Day. Ch'u Yüen was a wise counsellor and a poet. One day his wise advice was rejected by the leaders of China. Ch'u Yüen became very sad and wrote a poem called '**Li Sao**', which means '**Parting Sorrow**.' This poem told of his love for his country and in his sadness he then drowned himself in the river.

People rushed in boats to save him but could not do so. They tried throwing cooked rice into the water to stop the fish eating him.

One day a group of fishermen were out fishing and the ghost of Ch'u Yüen appeared. He told them to parcel rice in silk and tie the parcels with coloured threads, so that they would be protected against the water spirits.

Since then, people have held the boat races to remember the attempt to rescue Ch'u Yüen. They also eat rice dumplings which have been wrapped in leaves and tied with raffia. They hang sweet-smelling herbs at the tops of their doors and windows on the anniversary of his death. They believe that his spirit is still in the waters of rivers.

ALL ABOUT RICE

There are over 7,000 known varieties of rice and each grain of rice contains the beginnings of a new rice plant. It provides a basic diet for more than half of all the people in the world.

Rice grain has very little protein and fat, and contains 75 per cent starch. Most of the goodness lies in the husk, which contains salts and vitamins. The growing plants require a great deal of moisture, as well as scorching sun to ripen the grain. When the rice plants get a bit taller and stronger, they are transplanted into flooded fields, called **'paddy fields'**.

Rice flour contains only a little of the sticky gluten which enables wheat-flour to be made into dough, so it cannot be made into bread, but can be used for cakes and biscuits. The bran is used for feeding cattle.

Rice starch is another commercial product. Alcoholic drinks, such as saké and arrack, are made by fermenting the grain. Paper is made from the rice straw.

In India, rice is offered to the gods in celebration of thanksgiving, called '**pongal**'.

In Indonesia, the people worship the '**Rice Mother**'. It is believed that the first grains of rice were produced in the 'Rice Mother's' body, and that she watches over all the crops. The last sheaf of rice to be harvested is dressed as a woman in her honour.

In China they say you must finish all your rice because each grain represents the tears of China.

In Japan they build shrines to Inari, the '**rice-bearer**'.

THINGS TO DO

GROWING RICE

YOU WILL NEED

Small flower pots, 2 trays, peat, white and brown rice (see which one grows best).

METHOD

1. Fill a flower pots with peat. Sprinkle the rice on the surfaces and label them brown or white, and water. Make sure the pots are always damp.

2. Put some of the pots in a warm place, on a window sill or near a radiator. After a few days, some of the rice will begin to sprout.

3. When the rice plants get a bit taller and stronger, they are transplanted into flooded fields, called paddy fields. So transplant the pots into the trays.

PAINTING WITH RICE WATER

The water left over from cooking rice can be used to make invisible ink. The writing will show up when it is brushed over with iodine.

YOU WILL NEED

Rice water, paper, iodine, 2 containers

METHOD

1. Cook some rice and drain the water into a container and allow to cool.

2. Cut the paper into a boat shape and paint it with the rice water and allow to dry. Pour some iodine into a container and brush the boat with iodine.

A DRAGON BOAT

YOU WILL NEED

Plastic bottle, (one with a reinforced bottom), card 37 cm x 15 cm (15" x 6"), paint, water.

METHOD

1. Cut 10 cm (4") off the bottom of the bottle. Make a slit either side.

2. Cut out the dragon boat from the card as shown and paint it. Place the boat in the slits and float the boat in the water.

COOKING

STEAMED RICE DUMPLINGS

Traditionally, rice balls are wrapped in bamboo leaves and cooked in steam. In the middle of the balls are chopped peanuts, brown beans with sugar, fruit, or chopped meat. They are wrapped in bamboo leaves to keep them fresh and clean. Salted eggs are also eaten on the day of the Dragon Boat Festival.

<u>YOU WILL NEED</u>

100 g (4 oz) rice
50 g (2 oz) cooked chicken meat
25 g (1 oz) frozen peas, thawed
1 hard-boiled egg
salt and pepper

<u>METHOD</u>

1. Soak the rice in cold water overnight.

2. Next day, drain very well and grind it in a grinder or food processor.

3. Chop the chicken and hard-boiled egg very finely and add to the rice with the peas.

4. Form the mixture into eight small cakes.

5. Place each cake in the cups of an egg poacher. Fill the base with water. Poach the cakes for 10-12 minutes until set.

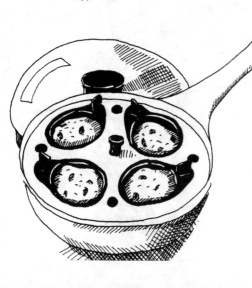

Suggested songs: Gao Trang Trang Trang, **Tum Tum June (Going around in a circle)** from **Songs that Children Sing**, by Eleanor Chorman, published by Oak Publications.

THE TORTOISE FAMILY

A tortoise can wander, very slowly, wherever it fancies because its home, the shell, is always right there. Of course it may eat up rather too much of its owner's garden in the process, so it's often a good idea to keep a tortoise in a wooden or wire-netting run.

A tortoise has no teeth, but it does have very sharp, horny jaws with which to cut up food.

Ideally, a tortoise should be allowed to feed freely, but if you are feeding it yourself remember that it particularly likes dandelion leaves, cabbage, clover, lettuce, and it may sometimes be tempted to take bread and milk. It also likes peas, beans, apple, pear, banana, and tomato. Food can be offered grated if too hard for the tortoise to bite.

During the winter a tortoise needs no attention at all, for it finds a leafy corner of the garden in which to hibernate, and there it stays for quite some time until the weather begins to look a little more inviting. When they rouse from hibernation, tortoises need to be cared for indoors for a few weeks to warm up. You can give your tortoise a warm bath in a shallow dish of clear water, and rub its shell with olive oil. As the weather improves, the tortoise can spend longer and longer in the garden, but will need to be boxed up at night until the danger of frost has passed.

In June or thereabouts, the female tortoise lays a clutch of about six eggs, and soon after buries them in any sunny spot she can find. The shell is soft on hatching, and very gentle handling is important.

Just as we have finger and hand prints, tortoises have different lines on their tummies. A system to identify tortoises has been created on a computer!

The tortoise and the turtle belong to the same family of reptiles, and at first glance they look alike. But they have different life styles, the turtle lives in the sea, only coming ashore to lay eggs, and it eats meat. The tortoise on the other hand, lives on dry land and feeds mainly on plants.

Terrapins are extremely active, they scuttle about on land, and swim rapidly using only the back legs. Their young are bright green with thin yellow lines on the head and neck, and a conspicuous red spot behind each ear.

Terrapins must be kept indoors in a vivarium heated to their preferred temperature range of 25 'C - 30 'C. Hatchlings need only shallow water, but adults require enough for fast swimming.

To create the dry land, place some rocks on one side of the vivarium. Then put some water in a separate container on the other side so that it can be cleaned easily. Place the vivarium where the sunlight can fall directly onto the terrapins.

Although mostly carnivorous, the red-eared terrapin will also take some green plant food. Small hatchlings should be given finely shreded red meat. Supplements such as fish liver oils may be given wrapped in tiny pieces of meat that will be swallowed before being tasted.

THE TORTOISE

A story to read

Tortoise loved his feet. They were so light that he could run faster than all the other animals. They were light because they didn't have any skin.

All the other animals said, 'You must get some skin.' But tortoise said, 'No, I like my feet.'

Every week they held a big race, and every week tortoise won. 'I always win,' shouted tortoise.

That night all the animals (except tortoise) held a meeting in the wood.

'We must get tortoise some skin,' said rabbit.

'I know, said spider, 'I will weave him some skin,' and she set off to weave the skin.

The next day, they told tortoise to put it on, and he did. At the next race the whistle blew, and they were off. But tortoise's skin was so heavy, that he lost.

By Simon West aged nine.

I HAVE A LITTLE TORTOISE

I have a little tortoise,
His name is Sunny Jim.
And when I roll him over,
He gives a little grin.

His shell is where his house is,
And he lives in my back yard.
But when I try to stroke him,
His shell is very hard.

THERE WAS A LITTLE TURTLE

There was a little turtle,
Who lived in a box.
He swam in a puddle,
He climbed on the rocks.
He snapped at a mosquito,
He snapped at a flea.
He snapped at a butterfly,
He snapped at me.
He caught the mosquito,
He caught the flea.
He caught the butterfly,
But he didn't catch me.

Anon

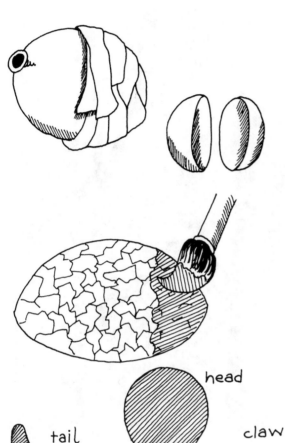

head

tail

claw

THINGS TO DO

MAKE A PAPER TORTOISE

YOU WILL NEED

Strips of paper, string, a balloon, wall paper paste (without anti-fungicide), broken egg shells or small sea shells, grey paint and PVA glue.

METHOD

1. Paste and cover the balloon with paper. Allow to dry in a warm place for a few days.

2. Cut the balloon in half, glue on the egg-shell, and paint with the grey paint. Poster paint is better if you use sea shells.

3. With the remaining half of the balloon cut out four claws, a tail, and a head. Place them on the body as shown. Tie the string to the tortoise so that the children can have a tortoise race.

FATHER'S DAY

Third Sunday in June

In 1909 Mrs. John Bruce Dodd of Spokane, Washington, had the idea of honouring her father, who had reared his six children on a Washington farm after his wife had died. She asked the Spokane Ministerial Association to set aside June 5th, her father's birthday, as the day for honouring fathers.

It was only in 1972 that a Congressional resolution permanently established the date as the third Sunday in June.

We celebrate Father's Day by giving gifts and having special treats for Fathers, but other countries which have a Father's Day often do it differently. In Czechoslovakia, for instance, Father's Day and Mother's Day both fall shortly before Christmas. On Father's Day the children tie the father onto a chair and sing, "Father's Day, Father's Day, What will you give?" Fathers give gifts to the children or they don't untie him!

THINGS TO DO

FATHER'S DAY CARD

<u>YOU WILL NEED</u>

Blotting paper, felt tips, saucer of water.

<u>METHOD</u>

Cut out the words HAPPY FATHER'S DAY, fold into a card as shown. Colour the words in with felt tips. Dip the bottom of the paper in the saucer of water. Leave it for a few minutes and watch the patterns appear.

COOKING

AMERICAN PIN WHEELS

<u>YOU WILL NEED</u>

225 g (8 oz) plain flour
50 g (2 oz) margarine
1/4 teaspoon bicarbonate of soda
1 teaspoon baking powder
pinch of salt
milk

Chocolate Mixture

50 g (2 oz) margarine
2 tablespoons sugar
1 dessert spoon of cocoa
1/2 teaspoon vanilla essence

Oven temperature: 170' C/325' F/Gas 3

<u>METHOD</u>

1. For the pastry, mix the flour, salt, soda, baking powder in a bowl. Rub in the margarine and bind to a stiff paste with the milk.

2. Cream margarine and sugar together, stir in the cocoa, add essence, and if necessary, a tablespoon of milk. Make sure the mixture isn't too soft or it will run during cooking.

3. Roll out the pastry into an oblong and spread with the chocolate mixture. Roll as for jam roll and cut into 2 cm (1") rounds. Place in a baking tin and bake for 20 to 30 minutes.

Suggested Songs: **Daddy Wouldn't Buy Me a Bow-Wow**, and **Going to the Zoo**, from **Apusskidu**, published by A. C. Black.

MIDSUMMER'S DAY

June 24th

Midsummer used to be celebrated with huge bonfires and torchlight processions in honour of the sun. It is thought that the fires were originally lit to worship the sun. Another theory is that the flames were supposed to ward off witchcraft. A fire was crowned with a broomstick, and a sickle with a newly cut oak handle was thrown into the flames to ensure the fertility of crops and men.

Midsummer's Eve was once believed to be a magic time, when ghosts, goblins and fairies became visible to ordinary mortals.

Many of the customs traditionally associated with Midsummer have now died away.

This day is also known as the festival of St John the Baptist.

GNOMES AND FAIRIES

In the garden you will find,
Gnomes and fairies of every kind.
When at night the stars peep out,
Watch them dancing and flitting about.

But if you see a butterfly,
Flying around in the evening sky.
Just stop, keep quiet, and see,
Because it might be a fairy flying free.

By Shirley West

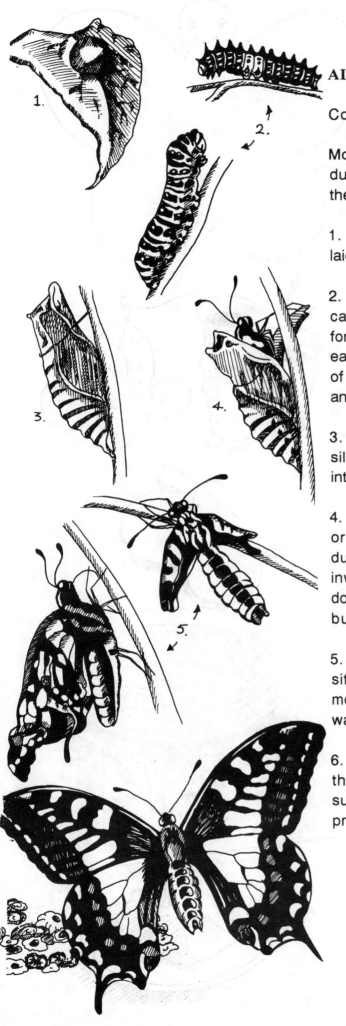

1.

2.

3.

4.

5.

ALL ABOUT BUTTERFLIES

Could butterflies really be fairies?

Most butterflies fly during the day and sleep during the night but with the moth it is often the reverse.

1. The butterfly starts its life as a tiny egg laid on plant leaves.

2. The eggs hatch into small larvae or caterpillars and spend the winter in this form. The caterpillar has nothing to do but eat. Food is stored up in the body in the form of fat, and is used to build up its wings, legs, and body.

3. Early in the summer, the caterpillar spins silk around itself to make a cocoon and turns into a pupa or chrysalis.

4. For some time (weeks or months) the pupa or chrysalis remains apparently asleep, but during this time it is gradually changing inwardly. The body of the caterpillar breaks down and reforms into the body of the butterfly.

5. When it first emerges from the chrysalis it sits still for a time, in order to let its thin, moist, crumpled wings spread out. Then it waves them slowly to dry them.

6. When its wings have expanded and dried, the new butterfly is ready to fly off into the summer sunshine in search of nectar-producing flowers and a mate.

THINGS TO DO

FAIRY BUTTERFLY PICTURES

YOU WILL NEED

A4 paper, 3 colours, string, 3 yoghurt pots, paint.

METHOD

1. Cut the paper into a butterfly shape with a face as shown. Cut 3 pieces of string.

2. Spoon the different coloured paints into the pot. Dip one piece of string into the paint then drop it onto the paper and move it around. Do the same with the other colours then fold in half.

BREEDING CATERPILLARS

YOU WILL NEED

Clear jar, muslin, rubber band, oasis, plant (the one you find the eggs on).

METHOD

1. Soak the oasis in some water and fix in the plant. Place this inside the jar and watch the caterpillars grow.

COOKING

BUTTERFLY FAIRY CAKES

It was believed that if you left little things such as nuts, raisins and perhaps little fairy cakes out in the garden for the fairies and gnomes, you would find it gone in the morning and a little crystal left in its place!

<u>YOU WILL NEED</u>

175 g (6 oz) self-raising flour
110 g (4 oz) castor sugar
110 g (4 oz) margarine
2 eggs, beaten
12 - 15 paper cases

For the Filling

110 g (4 oz) margarine
175 g (6 oz) icing sugar, sieved
almond essence

Oven temperature: 190 'C/375 'F/Gas 5

<u>METHOD</u>

1. Sift the flour. Cream the margarine and sugar until light and fluffy, then beat in the eggs a little at a time. Fold in the flour.

2. Spoon the mixture into the paper cases. Bake at the top of the oven for 15 - 20 minutes.

3. For filling, stir the sugar gradually into the margarine and add a few drops of essence.

4. When the cakes have cooled, cut a slice from the top of each and spoon in a generous amount of filling. Cut each cake slice in half and replace at an angle in the cream, to represent the butterfly's wings.

JULY

'Hot July brings cooling showers,
Apricots, and gillyflowers'.

Julius Caesar, the great Roman general, gave his name to July. Among the many things Caesar did was rearrange the Roman calendar. This gave Caesar a problem with the name of the original seventh month, which was previously called Quintilis meaning five. Caesar realized that it would be silly to have the seventh month with a name like the fifth, so he decided to call it after himself - and Julius became July.

AMERICAN INDEPENDENCE

July 4th

'We hold these truths to be self-evident; that all men are created equal; that they are endowed by their Creator with certain inalienable rights; that among these are life, liberty and the pursuit of happiness'.

From the Declaration of Independence, July 4th 1776, by Thomas Jefferson.

The Fourth of July is probably the most important day in the history of the United States of America and is a national holiday.

There is no school, and families celebrate together. Streets are hung with flags and decorations, and there are pageants and parades with fireworks in the evening.

The seeds of independence were sown in 1608 when John Smith founded the state of Virginia. The moves towards independence grew when the Pilgrim Fathers sailed in The Mayflower in 1620 to seek a country where they could practise their own faith which had been impossible in their Mother country. Other colonists followed from Ireland, France and Holland, as well as from England. Until the reign of George III there were thirteen colonies strung along the Atlantic coast of North America.

THINGS TO DO

4TH OF JULY HAT A marbling effect

<u>YOU WILL NEED</u>

2 sheets of A4 paper, red, white, and blue powder paint (or use glass paint), sunflower seed oil, tray, water, 3 containers, crépe paper.

<u>METHOD</u>

1. Mix each of the colours separately with some oil in the containers. Mix until the powder is absorbed into the oil and slightly runny.

2. Take a tray of cold water and drip a few drops of each colour on to it. It will float on the surface. Blow or lightly stir the water and this will create a marbling effect.

3. When the pattern is good, take the sheet of paper and drop it on the water then lift it off. Then repeat the process with the other sheet of paper. Allow to dry.

4. Tape the two pieces of paper together as shown to make the hat

5. Cut the crépe paper into thin strips and glue them to the hat as shown.

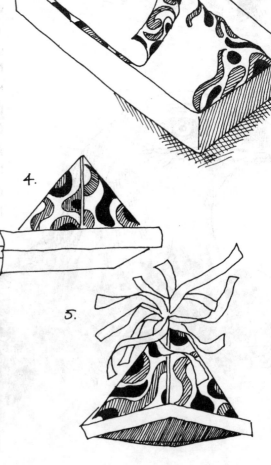

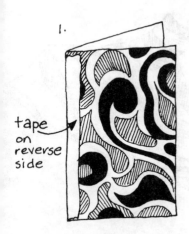

I.

tape
on
reverse
side

2.

3.

4.

5.

FIZZ AND FOAM

YOU WILL NEED

6 jars, two trays.

Place on a tray:

Acids

lemon juice
orange juice
2 crushed grapes

Place on a tray:

Carbonates

piece of chalk
bicarbonate if soda
crushed egg shell

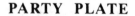

METHOD

1. Mix the lemon juice with the bicarbonate of soda and watch it fizz and foam.

2. Then try a combination of any of the other ingredients.

PARTY PLATE

YOU WILL NEED

Plate, petroleum jelly or oil, wall paper paste (without fungicide).

METHOD

1. Spread the petroleum jelly over a plate as a mould. Glue the paper to the plate and allow to dry for a few days. Once dry remove from the plate and trim ready for use.

COOKING

4TH OF JULY PARTY

YOU WILL NEED

Chicken drum sticks, sausages, sandwiches, red white and blue biscuits or cake, red jelly. Try and have as many red, white and blue things on the table as you can. Make American flags to place on the table.

CHEESE STRAWS

YOU WILL NEED

50 g (2 oz) cheese, grated
40 g (1 and 1/2 oz) margarine
75 g (3 oz) flour
salt and pepper
1/2 an egg yolk
a little water

Oven temperature: 200 'C/400 'F/Gas 4

METHOD

1. Grease a large, shallow, oblong tin. Sift the flour, salt and pepper and rub in the fat very lightly with the finger-tips. Add the grated cheese and mix well. Beat the egg with a little water and mix with the dry ingredients to form a stiff paste.

2. Knead the dough lightly until free from cracks, then turn onto a floured board and roll out into a strip about 10 cm (4") in width. Trim the edges, then cut across into narrow straws and place on the greased tin. Bake until golden-brown and firm to touch.

PEANUT BUTTER BISCUITS

YOU WILL NEED

110 g (4oz) self-raising flour
50 g (2oz) peanut butter
50 g (2 oz) margarine
50 g (2 oz) castor sugar
40 g (1 and 1/2 oz) light, soft brown sugar
40 g (1 and 1/2 oz) raisins
grated rind of 1/2 an orange
1 egg

Oven temperature: 180' C/350' F/Gas 4

METHOD

1. Cream together the peanut butter, orange rind, sugars and margarine until light and fluffy.

2. Beat the egg, add the raisins and stir in the flour to make a fairly firm dough. Roll the dough into small balls about the size of a walnut. Place well apart on a baking tray. Dip a fork in a little flour and press criss-cross lines on each ball. Bake in the centre of the oven for 25 minutes, until risen and golden-brown.

SHERBET FIZZ

YOU WILL NEED

2 spoons of citric acid crystals
1 spoon of bicarbonate of soda
6 spoons of icing sugar
any soft drink

METHOD

Add all the ingredients together to make the sherbet fizz.

TANABATA Japanese star festival

July 7th

July 7th is the festival of the Weaver-Maiden and the Cowherd, representing the two stars who were supposed to be able to meet on this day when they would cross the river in the sky, the Milky Way.

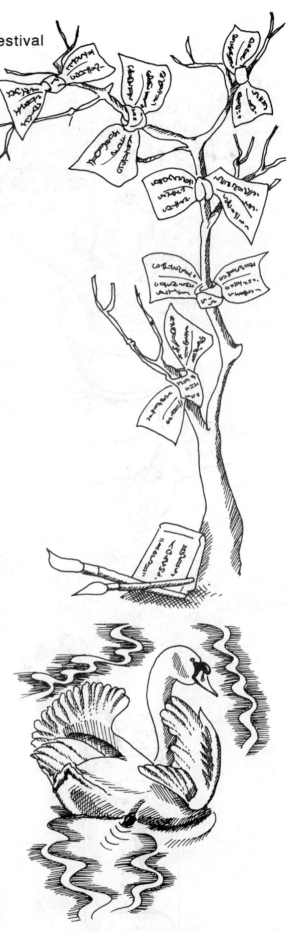

Many families display decorations made from **tanzaku** (a long strip of thick paper on which poems are written). These are attached to bamboo poles, and decorated with coloured paper streamers. Papier-mâché models of notebooks, brushes and other writing equipment are set up outside the house. It is, in a sense, a festival of literacy.

THE STORY OF TANABATA

Tanabata, which is on July 7th, is a festival celebrating the meeting of Orihime and Kengyu. They worked very hard, but when they met each other, they fell in love, and stopped working so well. The gods decided that since Orihime and Kengyu wouldn't work when they were near each other, they should be separated by a river known to us as Amanogowa (Milky Way). However, once a year, on July 7th, a swan would take them across the river to meet.

If you look in the sky on July 7th you will see the star Shocujo-sei, (Orihime), and star Kengyu-sei, (Kengyu), facing each other on either side of the Milky Way, with the star Hacucho-za, the swan, between them.

By Yudai Shiratori aged thirteen

THINGS TO DO

STAR RICE PAPER PICTURE

YOU WILL NEED

Tissues, PVA glue, water, black card, water colours, thin paint brush.

METHOD

1. Mix the glue with water until it is runny. Paint this slowly and carefully on to the tissue paper.

2. While it is still wet paint the tissue paper with the thin brush. Allow to dry then cut the paper into star shapes and mount the stars on to the black card.

TWINKLE TWINKLE

Twinkle, twinkle little star,
How I wonder what you are.
Up above the world so high,
Like a diamond in the sky.
Twinkle, twinkle little star,
How I wonder what you are.

As your bright and tiny spark,
Lights the traveller in the dark;
Though I know not what you are,
Twinkle, twinkle, little star.
Twinkle, twinkle little star,
How I wonder what you are.

By Jane Taylor

Suggested Songs: **On the River Flows**, from **Flying A Round**, published by A. C. Black.

THE MAD HATTER SAID TO THE QUEEN OF HEARTS

'Twinkle, twinkle, little bat!
How I wonder what you're at!
Up above the world you fly,
Like a tea tray in the sky.
Twinkle, twinkle, little bat!
How I wonder what you're at!'

From Lewis Carroll's **Alice in Wonderland.**

COOKING

SILVER STARS

<u>YOU WILL NEED</u>

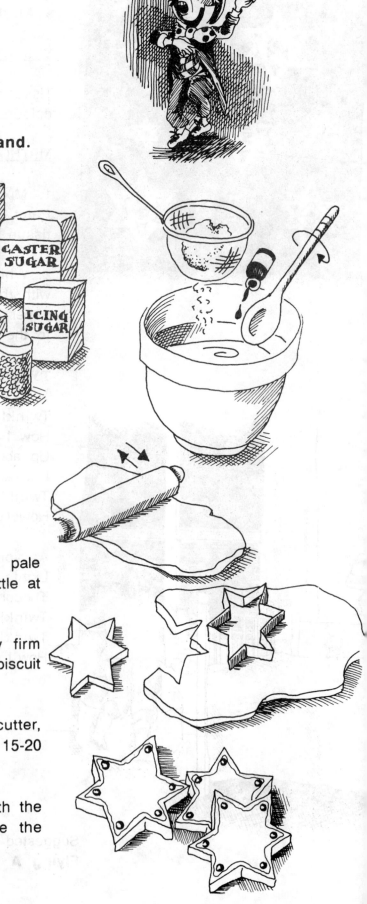

225 g (8 oz) plain flour
110 g (4 oz) margarine
110 g (4 oz) caster sugar
110 g (4 oz) icing sugar
1-2 tablespoons of warm water
a few drops of vanilla essence
1 egg, beaten   silver balls

Oven temperature: 180' C/350' F/ Gas 4

<u>METHOD</u>

1. Cream the margarine and sugar until pale and fluffy. Add the egg and essence a little at a time, beating after each addition.

2. Stir in the flour and mix to a fairly firm dough. Knead lightly and roll out to biscuit thickness.

3. Cut into stars, using a star-shaped cutter, and bake on a greased baking tray for 15-20 minutes.

4. Allow to cool. Mix the icing sugar with the warm water and ice the biscuits. Place the silver balls on the points of each star.

OUR UNIVERSE

Our universe consists of millions of galaxies distributed at random throughout space. Each galaxy contains thousands of millions of stars, interspersed with clouds of dust and gas, and gathered together in clusters.

The long irregular belt of white across the sky, called the Milky Way, is made up of myriads of stars which are so far away they look like a misty band. It can be seen, on a clear night, stretching in a tremendous arc from horizon to horizon.

The Earth is one of nine planets which spin around a star called the sun. Planets vary in size. Four are smaller than the Earth, these being Mercury (which is the closest to the Sun), Venus (which is closest to the Earth and is often thought of as its sister planet), Mars and Pluto (which is the smallest planet and farthest from the Sun).

Of the four larger ones: Jupiter is eleven times the diameter of Earth and has sixteen moons orbiting it; Saturn is the most beautiful, as it spins around with its rings like a top in the sky. Farther out in the solar system are Uranus and Neptune, each with a diameter nearly four times that of Earth.

Suggested Songs: **Battle of the Zartians**, from **Apusskidu**, published by A. C. Black.

THINGS TO DO

A PICTURE OF THE UNIVERSE

YOU WILL NEED

A very large sheet of paper, paint, paper cut into star shapes, paper cut into circles to represent the planets.

METHOD

Colours for the planets: Sun - red and orange, Mercury - grey and brown, Venus - white with streaks of black, Earth - blue and white, Moon - white, Mars - rusty red, Jupiter - light brown and white, Saturn - yellow with rings, Uranus and Neptune - turquoise, Pluto - light blue. Paint the large sheet of paper to represent the background for the planets.

Sun

Mercury

Earth
Moon

Venus

Mars

Saturn

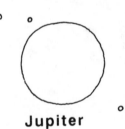

Jupiter

Uranus

Neptune

A MOON BASE FOR A ROCKET

YOU WILL NEED

Large sheet of thick card, egg shells, PVA glue, egg boxes (not the plastic ones), tin foil, kitchen roll tube, paint.

METHOD

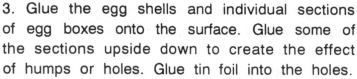

1. Paint the large sheet of card grey, black and white. Smear the colours for the right shadowy effect. Allow to dry.

2. For the rocket, paint the kitchen roll and allow to dry. Cut small pieces of tin foil and glue them to the rocket.

3. Glue the egg shells and individual sections of egg boxes onto the surface. Glue some of the sections upside down to create the effect of humps or holes. Glue tin foil into the holes.

A ROCKET IN THE SKY

See the rocket in the sky,
Flying, flying ever so high.
With a thrust and an almighty boom,
Speeding, speeding to reach the moon.

Now it's circling round a star,
Out in the deep black space so far.
Engines roaring full of light,
Out in the distant black of night.

Everyone's quiet, not saying a word,
Watching this giant silver bird.
Then with a thrust that late afternoon,
The rocket finally reaches the moon.

By Shirley West

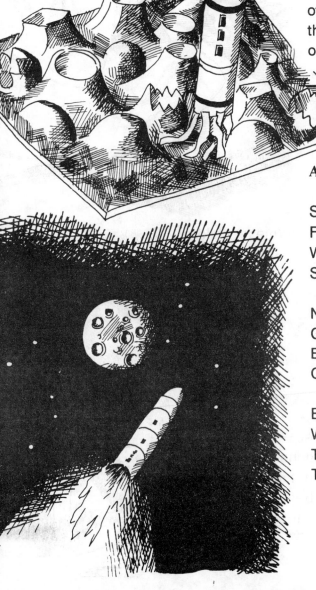

BON FESTIVAL

July 13th - 15th

Bon is known as the festival of lanterns. This is the time of year when the spirits of the dead return to visit the living. Buddhists in Japan remember their dead during this two-day festival.

Houses and graveyards are cleaned. At home, each family decorates a small altar, and food is placed on the altar for the spirits.

On the first evening a lighted lantern is placed at the door to welcome the spirits. Then everyone goes to the cemetery. The food and lighted lanterns are placed on the graves and the spirits are invited to join them.

On the last day, rice-balls are put out for the spirits to eat on their journey home. In the evening everyone gathers by the river. Small lanterns are lit and set on little water floats. The floats are cast off into the darkness of the night. The spirits are on their way back to the other world and everyone watches them drift slowly down the river.

BUDDHA AND THE SQUIRREL A tale told to Burmese children

Buddha, who had set out to search for truth, was so long in finding it that he decided that he should give up and return home. But on his way back he saw a squirrel sitting on the bank of a lake, dipping its tail into the water and shaking it over the land.

'Little squirrel,' said he, 'what are you doing?'
'I'm emptying this big lake,' replied the squirrel.
'But you will never be able to do that,' said Buddha.
'If you dipped your tail into the lake a million times there would still be nearly as much water as before.'
'Well,' said the squirrel, 'at least I would have tried.'

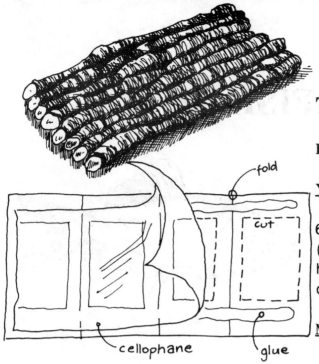

fold

cut

cellophane

glue

THINGS TO DO

FLOATING LANTERNS

<u>YOU WILL NEED</u>

6-8 twigs, wood glue, card 50 cm x 15 cm (20" x 6"), another strip of card for the handle 25 cm x 5 cm (10" x 2"), coloured cellophane.

<u>METHOD</u>

1. Glue the twigs together to form the raft.

2. Fold the card evenly into 4 sections. In each section cut out a 10 cm x 8 cm (4" x 3") oblong. Decorate the borders and the strip of card.

3. Cut the coloured cellophane into 12 cm x 8 cm (5" x 4") sizes and glue these to the inside of the lantern. Decorate and glue the handle.

THINGS THAT SINK OR FLOAT

Talk about things that sink or float.

<u>YOU WILL NEED</u>

Plasticine, tissues, sponge, pebbles, bowl of water.

<u>METHOD</u>

1. Experiment with plasticine by rolling it into a ball and dropping it in the water. Then take another piece of plasticine and shape it into a boat. Now see what happens!

2. Try using any of the other materials above and discuss with the children what happens to each of them.

ALL ABOUT GOLDFISH

'No human being, however great or powerful was ever so free as a fish.'

Ruskin

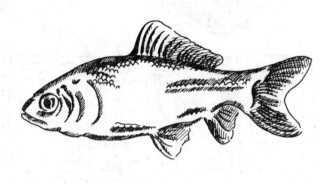

The common goldfish originated in East Asia and was greenish-bronze in colour. It was able to survive in water poor in oxygen, and to breed in small ponds. It has been kept as an ornamental fish for many centuries.

The best place for a goldfish is in an aquarium. Make sure they have sufficient oxygen and enough light (but not direct sunlight), that the water is not too cold, and that the fish are fed correctly. Fish breathe by extracting oxygen from the water passing through their gills - and the oxygen comes from the air on the surface of the water. So an aquarium should be as wide as possible at the top. Oxygen is also given off by plants, so water thyme or other pond weed should be planted in the gravel at the bottom. Newly-bought goldfish should not be plunged straight into cold tap water. Never put fish into the tank immediately after it has been planted and filled with water, they will not survive the shock. Allow the water to stand for a while and acquire the temperature of the room before the fish go in.

The aquarium should be kept where it will get plenty of daylight to keep the plants healthy, but avoid very strong sunlight as this encourages the growth of algae on the sides of the tank.

THINGS TO DO

A FISH PLAQUE

YOU WILL NEED

Cardboard 46 cm x 36 cm (18" x 14") for the background, cardboard 36 cm x 18 cm (14" x 7") for the fish shape, packet of polyfilla, paint, small sea shells or pebbles, plenty of yoghurt pots, mixing bowl, paint brush, sand, bottle tops.

METHOD

1. Paint the large card blue (do this the day before). Allow to dry. Draw a line 10 cm (4") from the bottom.

2. Mix the polyfilla in a bowl as instructed. This will stay workable for at least an hour.

3. Put small amounts of the mixture into several yoghurt cartons and then add different colours and mix well. Leave one plain.

4. Using the mixture paint the fish shape thickly using the fingers or a paint brush. Place the bottle tops over the fish.

5. Take the plain polyfilla and paint it at the bottom of the picture below the line. Sprinkle with sand and decorate with the shells.

FUN WITH MOTHBALLS

YOU WILL NEED

3 teaspoons white vinegar, dye, 2 teaspoons baking soda, glass jar, mothballs.

METHOD

1. Fill the jar with water, then slowly stir in the vinegar and baking soda. The liquid will start to fizz.

2. Add a few drops of dye, (not too much) and drop in the mothballs. The mothballs will sink to the bottom at first, but then they'll start to rise. When they reach the top of the liquid, they sink again.

You can get the same effect by dropping salted peanuts into a soft drink!

DANCING FISH

Weaving in and out,
In and out and diving.
Diving in the water,
Water of the seas,
Seas so blue and sparkling,
Sparkling and so bright,
Bright, sparkling fish,
Fish dancing in the night.

By Shirley West

Suggested Songs: **One two three four five**, from **Faber Book of Nursery Songs**, published by Oxford University Press. **Apusski Dusky**, from **Apusskidu**, published by A. C. Black. **Baby Sardines**, by Spike Milligan, from **Flying A Round**, published by A. C. Black.

EMPEROR HAILE SELASSIE 1

July 23rd

Emperor Haile Selassie 1 was born on July 23rd 1892, and this is one of the holiest days of the year for Rastafarians.

The original Rastafarians were Jamaicans led by a man called Marcus Garvey who was born in Jamaica in 1887 and believed to be the reincarnation of the prophet John the Baptist. He believed that black people were still suffering from the effects of slavery, and he encouraged thousands of black people in Jamaica and America to unite and take pride in their African heritage.

Haile Selassie 1 became Emperor of Ethiopia on November 2nd in 1930. Before he became Emperor his title was Ras Tafari. '**Ras**' means prince or head and '**Tafari**' means creator. He was seen as the King prophesied by Marcus Garvey.

Ethiopia was attacked and overrun by Italy in 1935, and Haile Selassie went into exile until the British Forces drove the Italians out in 1941. On his return he modernised the government, established schools throughout the country, and abolished slavery.

In 1974 he was deposed in a military coup. He was accused of neglecting the peasants during the long drought.

He was accepted as the living God and many people do not believe he has died. It is believed that when death does occur it is a trick of Babylon. The spirit of the dead person will resist the trickery and be reincarnated elsewhere.

Rastafarian beliefs are based on the Bible. They follow a passage in the Bible which says:

'They shall not make baldness upon their head, neither shall they shave off the corner of their beard...' (Leviticus Ch.21, V.5.).
Instead of cutting their hair, they twist it into shapes which are meant to make people feel respect for them. The Rastafarian name for this respect is '**dread**', which is why they call this kind of hair '**dreadlocks.**'

In prayer they shape their hands to symbolize both peace and war. This represents a heart and a spear. God is called '**Jah**' and they believe that God always spoke of himself as '**I**'. So when Rastafarians speak of themselves they say '**I and I**' meaning that they are at one with God. They believe there is no God outside themselves for God the Father is within them.

Rastafarians use the Ethiopian calendar. This has 13 months in a year and begins on September 11th. The last month of the year has only six days and each year is named after one of the apostles - Matthew, Mark, Luke and John. 1991 is the year of Mark.

Reggae music plays an important role because it is seen as a mark of their identity. The words describe Rastafarian oppression, exile, beliefs, suffering and a longing for home. There are three main drums. These are the bass (the sound of thunder), fundie (the sound of an earthquake), and repeater (the sound of lightning). When they come together to drum and chant it is called **Nyahbinghi**. Nyahbinghi was an order, believed to have been founded by Haile Selassie, which is pledged to end oppression in society - black or white.

THE LION OF JUDAH

Rastafarians believe that Haile Selassie, Lion of Judah, united the human and the animal world. He was fearless, and lions roamed his garden and slept at his feet. The proud walk of the lion is copied by Rastamen, and a lion symbol is featured in their art.

The colours green, yellow, and red representing the Ethiopian flag are often included in paintings.

Red is seen as the colour of strength, the blood of the patriots, or faith. Yellow is for the church, peace, natural wealth, or love. Green is seen as a symbol of the land and hope.

THINGS TO DO

THE LION OF JUDAH

<u>YOU WILL NEED</u>

Large paper, green, yellow, and red paint.

<u>METHOD</u>

1. Cut the large piece of paper into a lion shape.

2. Draw 12 cm (5") wide lines as shown. Paint alternately with the colours above.

Another idea is to make Ethiopian flags.

THREE DRUMS

<u>YOU WILL NEED</u>

lightning - tin foil and cling film
thunder - container with the lid on
earthquake - thick card, pulses
rubber bands, 3 tins or large empty plastic
containers, 2 wooden spoons.

<u>METHOD</u>

1. Cut three layers of tin foil and place on top of the container. For more protection cover with cling film and secure with a rubber band. Tap lightly with the fingers.

2. Drum the lidded container with the lid on with one of the wooden spoons.

3. Put a handful of pulses into a container. Cut enough card to overlap the top of the container and secure it down with a rubber band. Drum with a wooden spoon.

THREE RATTLES

<u>YOU WILL NEED</u>

3 toilet rolls, paper, beans, rice, bells, green, yellow, and red paint, glue.

<u>METHOD</u>

1. Cut enough paper to cover toilet roll. Before covering add the different sounds.

2. Secure the ends with glue and paint each one a different colour.

Coconut halves can be used as a musical instrument by banging them together.

COOKING

I-TAL

Rastafarians are mainly vegetarians and so do not eat pork, shellfish, or any other fish over 18 cm (7") long . These rules are found in the Old Testament. No rum, milk or coffee may be drunk, only fruit juice. They do not salt their food. So I-Tal means food that is natural and clean.

COCONUT BUNS

YOU WILL NEED

110 g (4 oz) vegetable margarine
175 g (6 oz) raw cane sugar
175 g (6 oz) freshly grated coconut
275 g (10 oz) wholemeal flour
2 teaspoons baking powder
1/2 teaspoon ground cinnamon
150 ml (5 fl oz) milk

Pre heated oven temperature: 180' C/350' F Gas 4

METHOD

1. Cream the margarine and raw cane sugar until well blended. Sift the flour, baking powder and ground cinnamon in a separate bowl. Stir in the coconut.

2. Add the dry ingredients alternately with the milk to the creamed mixture. Divide the mixture and shape into buns with floured hands.

3. Place the buns on a greased baking tray, spacing them well apart, and bake in the oven for 25 minutes or until risen and brown.

RICE AND PEAS

YOU WILL NEED

175 g (6 oz) gungo peas or black-eye beans
225 g (8 oz) brown rice
150 ml (5 fl oz) coconut milk
1 sprig thyme
freshly ground black pepper

METHOD

1. Soak the dried peas or beans in plenty of cold water overnight.

2. Drain and place in a pan with enough cold water to cover and bring to the boil, cover and simmer for about an hour until the peas are tender.

3. Add the washed rice to the pan together with the coconut milk and a seasoning of thyme and freshly ground pepper. Add extra water to bring the level of liquid in the pan to just above the rice.

4. Cook on a low heat for a further 20-25 minutes by which time all the liquid should be absorbed and the rice soft.

Suggested Songs: **Oh, we can play on the big bass drum**, from **Okki-Tokki-Unga**, **Island in the sun, Lazy coconut tree, Mango walk, Jamaica farewell, from Ta-ra-ra boom-de-ay**, all published by A. C. Black.

AUGUST

'August brings the sheaves of corn;
The harvest home is borne'

The Romans used to call August Sextilis, the sixth month. But when Julius Caesar reformed the calender the name no longer suited it. Finally the Romans changed it to August to honour and flatter their Emperor Augustus, grand-nephew of the great Caesar.

THE SUN

From earliest time, people realised the sun's importance to the Earth. But they did not know all that we know about it and many worshipped it as a god.

They found various ways of explaining its daily journey across the sky. The Greek sun god, Helios, drove his chariot across the sky. The Egyptian sun god, Re, sailed his boat: he was young when he set out at dawn, grown up by noon, and old at sunset when he arrived in the west.

In America, the Indians used to hold a sun dance lasting several days. The men painted their bodies and danced facing the sun, to the music of whistles made of eagle bone.

Centuries ago the Incas in Peru called themselves children of the sun, and performed strange ceremonies in worship of the king of the heavenly bodies. They may have been mistaken in thinking the sun was a god, but they were right in believing that there would be no earth and no people if it were not for the sun. If the light of the sun were shut off, everyone would perish from cold and starvation.

The coal that people burn comes from the sun. Coal was formed from giant ferns and other primitive plants which long ago stored up the rays of sunlight.

Suggested Songs: **I Watch the Sunrise**, from **Alleluya**, published by A. C. Black.

THINGS TO DO

SUNFLOWERS

The North American Indians cultivated these flowers. The stalks furnished the Indians with a textile fibre, its leaves served as fodder, its flowers yielded a yellow dye, and its seeds provided both food and oil.

The sunflower sometimes reaches a height of 10 feet. Each **'head'** produces a large number of seeds, rich in fat and protein, which are fed to poultry and livestock or are crushed for their oil. In some countries the seeds are roasted and eaten. Its name derives from the fact that the flower-heads turn in the sun's direction.

YOU WILL NEED

Paper, yellow paint, lentils, PVA glue, A4 paper.

METHOD

1. Make hand prints with yellow and allow to dry. Cut the hand prints out.

2. For the stem roll the sheet of A4 paper length-ways, as tight as possible, and paint yellow.

3. Cut out a circle 12 cm (5") in diameter, paint yellow and allow to dry. Glue the lentils to the circle.

4. Glue the hand prints to the back of the circle to form the petals. Staple the stem to the back of the sunflower.

VANISHING WATER

Water doesn't really disappear when it dries up. Tiny droplets of water rise into the air, but they are so small that you cannot see them. One way to show the children how this happens is to boil a kettle and watch the steam rise and disappear.

YOU WILL NEED

Two jars, strip of paper, rubber band, 4 cups of water.

METHOD

1. Using the rubber band, fasten the strip of paper on the outside of jar **A**. Pour in one cup of water and leave open.

2. Pour one cup of water into jar **B** and screw the lid on tightly. Put both the jars on a sunny window sill and leave them for a few days. Mark the level of the water in jar A every day. What happens to the water in jar B?

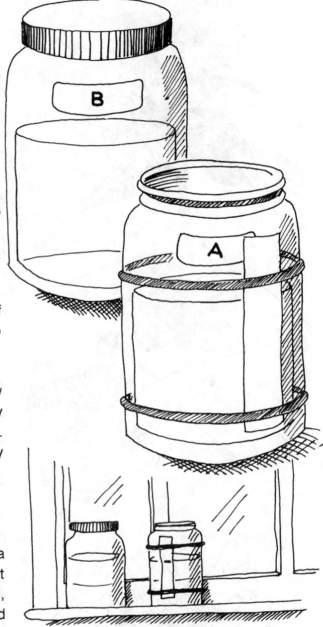

PAINTING WITH WATER

On a hot summer's day, give the children a plastic container with water and a paint brush. Let them paint paving stones, walls, trees and flowers. Hours of fun can be had painting then watching the water disappear.

Find a puddle in the playground and draw a chalk line round it. Draw around the puddle again every half hour and chart how fast it dries up.

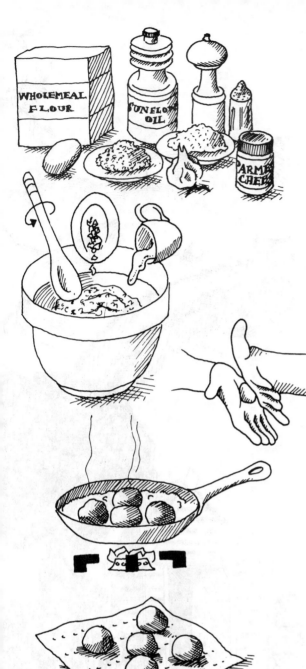

COOKING

SUNFLOWER SNACKS

<u>YOU WILL NEED</u>

110 g (4 oz) sunflower seeds, ground
110 g (4 oz) fresh wholewheat breadcrumbs
50 g (2 oz) wholemeal flour
2 tablespoons grated Parmesan cheese
salt and pepper
1 clove garlic, crushed
1 large egg, lightly beaten
oil for frying

<u>METHOD</u>

1. Mix together the ground sunflower seeds, breadcrumbs, Parmesan, a little salt and pepper in a bowl.

2. Stir in the garlic, then add the beaten egg and mix well to bind the ingredients together.

3. Using floured hands, roll the mixture into small balls. Dip each ball into some flour and coat thoroughly. Heat the oil for deep-frying and fry the balls in batches until crisp and golden. Drain on absorbent kitchen paper.

SUNFLOWER SEED SPREAD

<u>YOU WILL NEED</u>

110 g (4 oz) sunflower seeds, ground
50 g (2 oz) peanut butter
1-2 tablespoons vegetable oil

<u>METHOD</u>

Mix together the ground sunflower seeds and peanut butter. Add some oil to get the required consistency for spreading onto bread.

RAINBOWS

THE RAINBOW LADY

A story to read

It had stopped raining and Leanna put on her wellies and ran to the end of the garden, where she had her secret hide-out. It was just a tumbled down shed, but she had tried to make it pretty by putting a few of her paintings on the walls. Leanna had an old mattress on the floor whereupon sat her favourite doll, Henbin. He had black hair and a funny smile on his face.

While Leanna was combing his hair she heard a strange noise, coming from outside. 'Who could it be?' she thought, 'It can't be Henbin because he's here with me.' She went outside to see. She stopped suddenly and stared, for there behind a stone was a strange figure.

'Who are you?' stuttered Leanna. 'I'm, I'm, 'I'm the Rainbow Lady,' she sobbed. 'But why are you crying?' asked Leanna. 'Can't you see all my colours have faded and the sun won't come out, so I can't reach the sky.'

'But why do you need the sun?' asked Leanna. 'Don't you know? can't you see? I have no colour in my rainbow unless the sun shines on me,' she sobbed again.

The Rainbow Lady stopped crying and looked at Leanna. 'You see she,' explained, 'the sunlight falls on my droplets of rain, and when that happens, the light is bent as it enters each drop.'

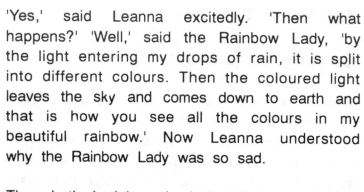

'Yes,' said Leanna excitedly. 'Then what happens?' 'Well,' said the Rainbow Lady, 'by the light entering my drops of rain, it is split into different colours. Then the coloured light leaves the sky and comes down to earth and that is how you see all the colours in my beautiful rainbow.' Now Leanna understood why the Rainbow Lady was so sad.

They both hadn't noticed the Rain Man hiding behind the trees. He had been listening all the time.

'Well,' said the Rain Man, 'I shall go and talk to the sun and see what I can do for you.' 'Oh! thank you,' said the Rainbow Lady.

The Rain Man found the sun hiding behind a cloud. 'Well,' said the Rain Man, 'what's this I've been hearing? Don't you know that all us weather people must take our turn in providing weather for this earth? And here you are hiding behind a cloud! What have you got to say for yourself?'

'It's not my fault,' said the sun. 'This cloud is stuck in front of me.' 'Oh, that's easy,' said the Rain Main. And he started to slowly push the cloud out of the sun's way. 'That's better, now I can shine for all the world to see,' said the sun.

Just at that moment the Rainbow Lady was free to climb into the sky and form her arc of beautiful colours. Leanna gazed up into the sky and said to Henbin, 'I'm the only one in the world who knows how a rainbow is made, aren't I?'

By Shirley West

Suggested Songs: **Sing A Rainbow**, from **Apusskidu**, published by A. C. Black. **Raindrops keep fallin' on my head, Rain and sun, What have they done to the rain?**, from **Alleluya**, published by A. C. Black.

THINGS TO DO

RAINBOW IN A BUBBLE

Different colours can be seen because when the light hits a bubble, most of it passes through, because the bubble is transparent. But as the air in it evaporates and the bubble gets even thinner, some of the rays that make up white light don't pass through. Instead, they are reflected back from either the inside or the outside.

YOU WILL NEED

A jar of soapy water, a teaspoon of sugar, 4 tablespoons of glycerine or vegetable oil, straw or a bubble blower (this can be made from wire), cloth.

METHOD

1. Make four slits, each about 1 cm (1/2") long, in one end of the straw.

2. Fill the jar two-thirds full of warm soapy water. Add the sugar and vegetable oil. Shake vigorously. Strain the liquid through a cloth and cool in the refrigerator for a few minutes. This will make the bubbles last longer.

3. Dip the bubble blower into the liquid and blow gently.

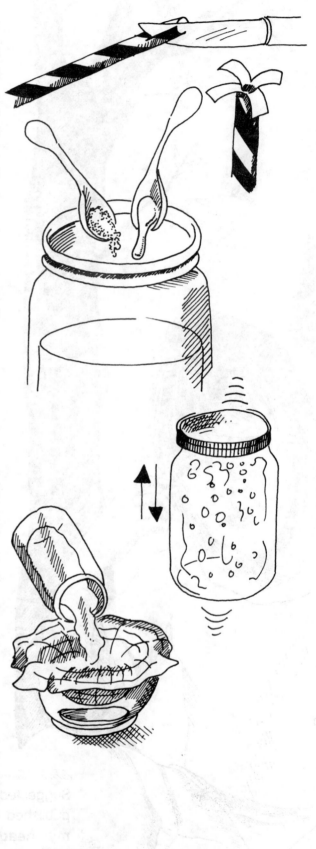

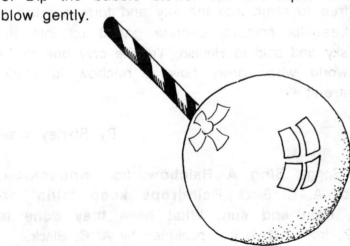

PAINT THE COLOURS OF A RAINBOW

YOU WILL NEED

Runny paint in red, orange, yellow, green, blue, indigo, and violet, large sheet of paper, straws.

METHOD

1. Spread a tablespoon of red paint in a long line at the top of the paper. Place the end of the straw near the paint and blow gently dispersing the paint upwards.

2. Next spread the orange paint below the red and follow step 1. Do the same with all the colours in the order listed above.

COLOURED VIEWERS

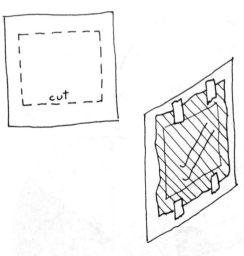

YOU WILL NEED

4 square cards, 4 pieces of cellophane in different colours, sticky tape.

METHOD

1. Cut a window as shown in each of the cards and tape the different coloured cellophane onto each of the cards.

2. If you can find a pen the same colour as one of the cellophanes, draw a picture on a piece of paper. Then put the coloured viewer over the picture and see what happens.

A KALEIDOSCOPE

YOU WILL NEED

Scraps of different coloured cellophane, clear cellophane, a highly glazed post card, glue.

METHOD

1. Divide the long side along its length as shown into four sections and scratch the lines lightly. Glue the card into a triangular tube-shape with the glazed side facing inwards.

2. Glue both ends with the clear cellophane. Place the small scraps of cellophane on top of one of the clear ends and cover with a piece of white paper. Make sure it is loose enough for the scraps to move easily.

3. Look through the clear end and tap lightly. Each time you tap a new pattern will appear.

DISAPPEARING COLOURS

YOU WILL NEED

Card cut into a circle 12 cm (5") in diameter, red, orange, yellow, green, blue, and violet paint, a pencil.

METHOD

1. Divide the circle into six equal sections. Paint each one in the order above. Allow to dry.

2. Punch a hole in the centre of the circle. Push a sharp pencil through the hole and spin.

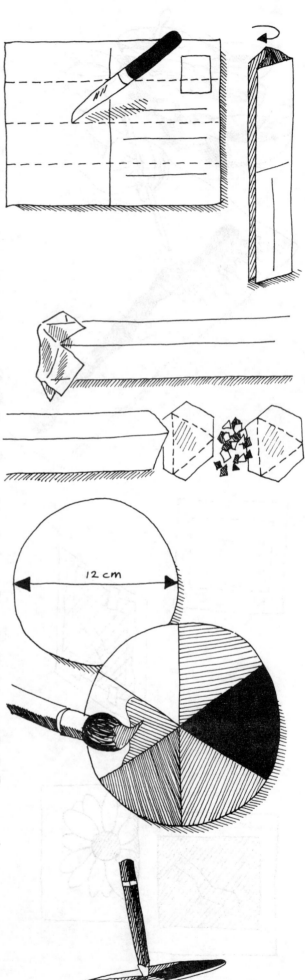

noon

6 a.m.   6 p.m.

SHADOWS

On a sunny day, shadows are formed by anything that blocks the sun's rays.

When you stand in the sun, your body stops some of the sun's rays from reaching the ground.

Shadows shrink and grow during the day according to the sun's position in the sky. Around midday the sun is overhead: its rays shine down directly onto your head and shoulders, and casts almost no shadow, or a very small one. In the early morning and evening the sun shines low in the sky: its rays slant towards you, striking the full length of your body and casting a long shadow.

THINGS TO DO

SHADOW PUPPETS

A delightful account of the invention of shadow puppets is given in the tale of the Emperor Wu-Tu (121 B.C.) of the Han Dynasty. Distraught by the death of someone he loved dearly, he commanded the court magician to summon her spirit to return to him. The magician satisfied the Emperor by producing at the far end of a darkened room a shadow on a screen which resembled his girlfriend.

Shadow play were given by Punch and Judy showpeople in the 1830s, who stretched calico across the punch booth at night, and gave shadow puppet shows known as Galanty shows.

TRICKS WITH SHADOWS

YOU WILL NEED

Dark room, white wall or a large sheet of white paper, table, powerful torch.

METHOD

1. Place different objects on the table in a line. For example a plastic bottle, water in a jar with something floating in it.

2. Bring the torch closer to the objects and see what happens. The shadow will get bigger.

HAND SHADOWS

YOU WILL NEED

dark room, white wall or a large sheet of white paper, powerful torch

METHOD

Follow the hand positions as shown.

Crocodile

Geese

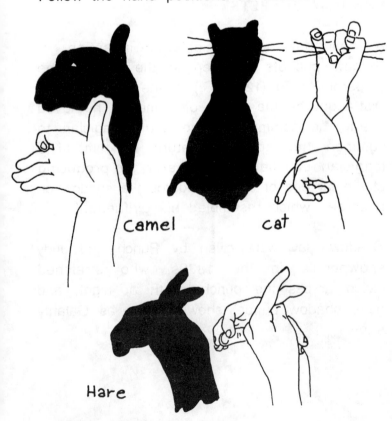

Camel

cat

Hare

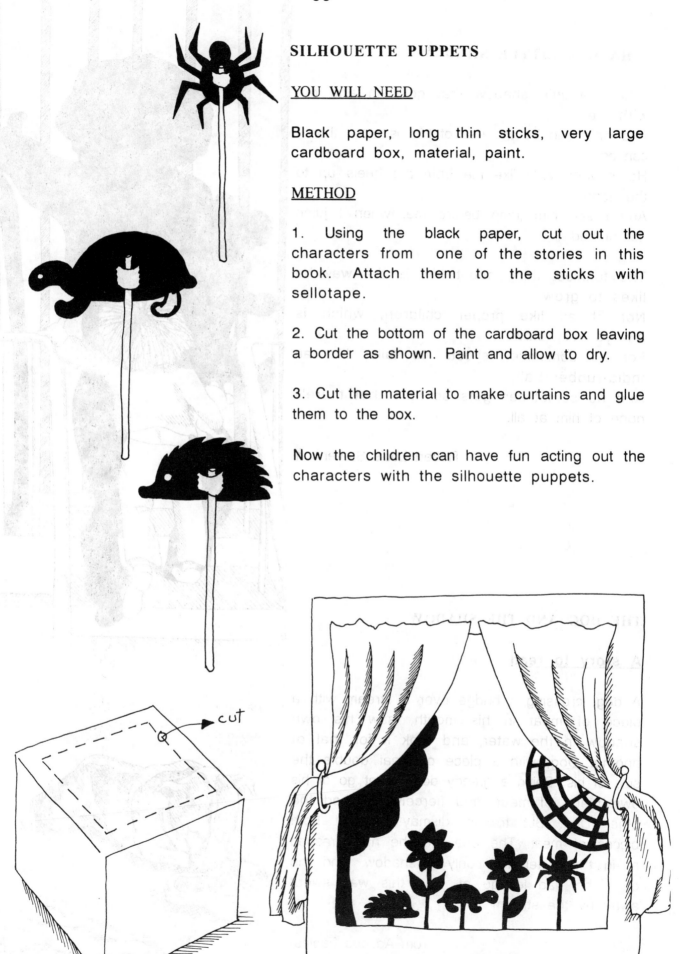

SILHOUETTE PUPPETS

YOU WILL NEED

Black paper, long thin sticks, very large cardboard box, material, paint.

METHOD

1. Using the black paper, cut out the characters from one of the stories in this book. Attach them to the sticks with sellotape.

2. Cut the bottom of the cardboard box leaving a border as shown. Paint and allow to dry.

3. Cut the material to make curtains and glue them to the box.

Now the children can have fun acting out the characters with the silhouette puppets.

I HAVE A LITTLE SHADOW

I have a little shadow that goes in and out
with me,
And what can be the use of him is more than I
can see.
He is very, very like me from the heels up to
the head;
And I see him jump before me, when I jump
out of bed.

The funniest thing about him is the way he
likes to grow-
Not at all like proper children, which is
always very slow;
For he sometimes shoots up taller like an
India-rubber ball,
And he sometimes gets so little that there's
none of him at all.

Robert Louis Stevenson

THE DOG AND THE SHADOW

A story to read

A dog, crossing a bridge over a stream with a
piece of meat in his mouth, saw his own
shadow in the water, and took it for that of
another Dog, with a piece of meat double the
size of his. Being a greedy dog he let go of his
own piece of meat, and fiercely attacked the
other Dog. But to his dismay he lost both
pieces of meat. The one that he had grasped
at in the water was only a shadow. And the
other he had let go of, and this was swept
away by the stream.

From Aesops Fables.

RAKSHA BANDHAN

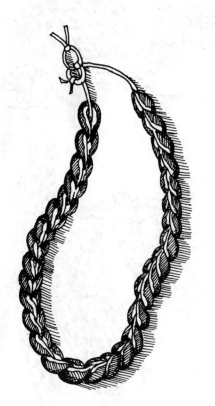

July/August

This is a festival for brothers and sisters in the family and is celebrated by both Hindus and Sikhs. It falls on the day of the full moon in the Hindu month Shravana, which generally coincides with July or August. Sisters tie Rakshabandham (meaning to tie for security), which is also known as Rakhi, on their brother's wrist. They also mark their brother's forehead with vermilion (bright scarlet) powder. This powder is used as a symbol of success and victory. Rakhi is made from red and gold silk thread. The gift of the bracelet shows the sister's love for her brother. By wearing the bracelet, the brother promises to protect her for ever.

There are many stories associated with Raksha Bandhan, one of which tells how, during the Muslim rule, a beautiful Hindu Queen called Padmini sought protection from the Mughal Emperor by sending him a Rakhi. Later Padmini was threatened by another Muslim King who was determined to marry her after seeing her reflection in a mirror. But the Queen was defended against this invasion by the Mughal Emperor in response to the Rakhi she had sent.

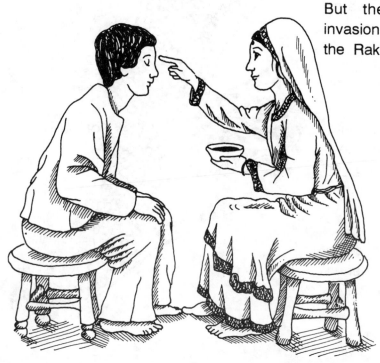

THINGS TO DO

HENNA HAND AND FEET PAINTING

Mehndi (henna) is used at festival times and for decoration in Pakistan and some parts of India.

Henna designs are very intricate and beautiful. Henna dyes the skin a deep red-brown colour and the design lasts for a couple of weeks. Henna is a herb and can be used to protect the skin and can be put in shampoo as a conditioner.

Only brides have the tops of the feet and hands painted. The longer they leave the henna on the darker it gets.

YOU WILL NEED

Henna powder, lemon juice, warm water, oil of eucalyptus, sugar, thin paint brush or stencils, bowl, cotton wool.

METHOD

1. Put a few teaspoons of henna powder into a bowl and add a little lemon juice and warm water to make a fluid paste. Mix thoroughly.

2. Leave it to stand in a warm place for a couple of hours.

3. Rub a few drops of oil of eucalyptus onto the palm of the hand. Using the thin paintbrush paint a pattern on the hand or alternatively place the stencil on the hand and paint over it.

4. If needed, thin the henna powder with some warm water. Allow to dry. To stop the henna flaking off, dab a mixture of sugar and lemon juice over the design with cotton wool.

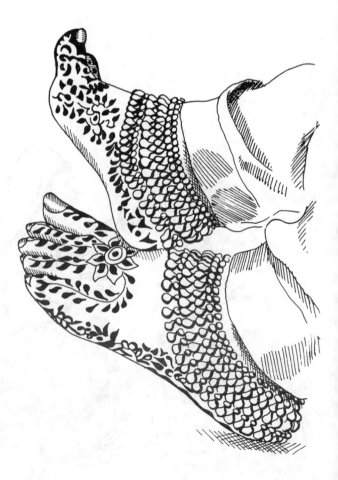

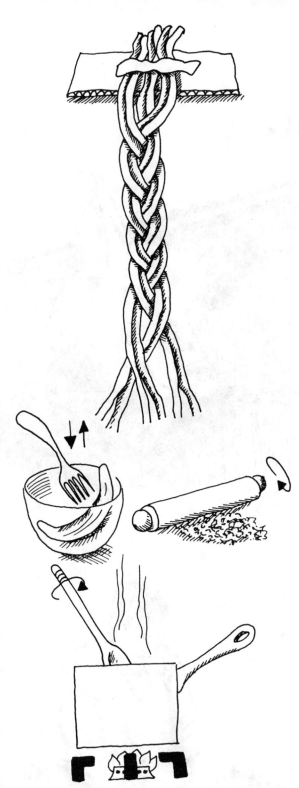

WOOL BRACELET

<u>YOU WILL NEED</u>

Three different colours of wool, small piece of cardboard, sellotape.

<u>METHOD</u>

Cut two of each colour into 12 cm (5") lengths. Secure the six ends of the wool to the cardboard with the sellotape. Start to plait two strands at a time. Remove from the card and tie round the wrist.

COOKING

Hindus often give presents of sweetmeats at their special festivals.

INDIAN BANANA FUDGE

<u>YOU WILL NEED</u>

50 g (2 oz) ground almonds
50 g (2 oz) brown sugar
50 g (2 oz) semolina
25 g (1 oz) margarine   3 cardamom pods
1 large banana   4 tablespoons of water

<u>METHOD</u>

1. Mash the banana with a fork and keep to one side. Remove the seeds from the cardamom pods and crush them with a rolling pin. Add to the bananas.

2. Melt the margarine and gently fry the semolina until it turns golden in colour. Stir in the bananas, ground almonds, sugar, and water. Bring to the boil and cook, stirring all the time, until the mixture comes away from the sides of the pan. Spoon into a shallow greased tin and place in the fridge to set. Cut into small squares.

FOOD AND FARMING

FARM ANIMALS

Animals were domesticated thousands of years ago. First sheep and goats, and then later pigs and cattle. Selective breeding has transformed their appearance, turning the hairy, long-legged wild boar into the fat, smooth-skinned domestic pig, and the wild ox into the cow.

Summer is a pleasant season not only for farm animals, but for us as well. Most will enjoy the warm sunshine and plenty of food.

But there are two farm animals who don't take kindly to the hot weather. Firstly pigs, who have no thick hair or fur to protect them from the sun and can suffer severely from sunburn if they cannot find shade. Best of all, they like a muddy pool to wallow in. Secondly sheep. They are mountain animals and grow very thick coats of wool, known as fleeces, to protect them from frost and blizzards of winter. In summer wild sheep will retreat up the mountains to where it is cooler. But sheep on the farm can't do this, so the farmer shears off their thick winter fleece at the start of summer. This wool is an important farm product and is used for weaving into clothes. Sheep-shearing is regarded as a kind of festival in some countries, such as Wales and New Zealand. Farming families gather to help each other with the shearing and afterwards join together to have a feast.

One of the chief irritations for animals in summer are stinging and biting insects, which are plentiful at this time of year. On hot days you will often see cattle and horses swishing their tails, as they try to shake off flies and other pests.

A VISIT TO A FARM

Just as human beings are known as man, woman or child, according to sex and age, so too do animals have special names to distinguish them.

ANIMAL	FEMALE	MALE	JUVENILE
Birds	hen	cock	chick
Cattle	cow	bull	calf
Deer	doe	buck	fawn
Dog	bitch	dog	puppy
Donkey	jennet	donkey	foal
Duck	duck	drake	duckling
Fox	vixen	fox	cub
Goat	nanny	billy	kid
Goose	goose	gander	gosling
Hare	doe	buck	leveret
Horse	mare	stallion	foal
Pig	sow	boar	piglet
Sheep	ewe	ram	lamb
Swan	pen	cob	cygnet

OTHER ANIMALS

	FEMALE	MALE	JUVENILE
Bear	she-bear	bear	cub
Elephant	cow	bull	calf
Kangaroo	doe	buck	Joey's
Lion	lioness	lion	cub
Seal	cow	bull	pup
Tiger	tigress	tiger	cub
Whale	cow	bull	calf

Suggested Songs: **Six Little Ducks**, from **Okki-Tokki-Unga**, **One Potato, Two Potato**, and **The Animals Went in Two by Two**, from **Ta-ra-ra boom-de-ay**, all published by A. C. Black.

FARMING FOOD

Once people found all their food by hunting animals and gathering wild fruits and vegtables. Today the production and distribution of food is a huge industry. Nature has been tamed, and wild animals domesticated. The only food that is still hunted is fish, and even there, fish are being farmed in ponds.

Most people want food to be as cheap as possible and intensive production gives the cheapest meat and eggs. No human being would want to live the way some farm animals are forced to live.

The majority of hens are kept indoors with groups of four of five in each cage. Rows of cages are stacked in batteries of three or four tiers. Conveyor belts in front of the cages collect the eggs and supply the feed, and a conveyor under each tier removes the droppings. Lights are used to extend the length of the day so that the hens lay eggs in the winter.

Pigs are usually raised indoors, kept in pens and fed a special diet to make them grow quickly.

A modern milking parlour is like a factory production line. Cows stand in rows with machinery attached to their udders and their milk automatically passes to a temperature-controlled tank.

Many people have become vegetarians and get all the nourishment they need by eating nuts, beans, grains, fruit and vegetables.

barley rye oats

CEREALS

Cereals are the most important crops, and they belong to the grass family. Wheat, rice, maize, barley, oats and rye are the six principal cereal crops, providing about half of our food energy and much of our essential protein and vitamins too. Wheat and rice, on a world scale, are the two most important cereals.

THINGS TO DO

MAKE A WINDMILL

The original purpose of a windmill was to use the force of wind to grind corn or to pump water. The revolving sails were used to turn millstones between which corn was ground into flour. There are now speedier ways of grinding corn. Today, windmills are used for the generation of electricity.

<u>YOU WILL NEED</u>

A box 23 cm x 15 cm (9" x 6"), a 20 cm (8") square piece of paper, paint, an old magazine, paper clip, coloured shapes.

<u>METHOD</u>

1. Paint the box and allow to dry. Cut a door and windows from the magazine and glue onto the box.

2. Take the square piece of paper and cut along the dotted line as shown. Stick on the coloured shapes. Then turn each right hand corner into the centre, and glue.

A FARM YARD SCENE

YOU WILL NEED

Different shaped cereal boxes, paint, cotton wool, very large cardboard box, white card, paper, PVA glue, small twigs.

METHOD

1. Cut out the bottom of the large cardboard box and paint it green. Allow to dry.

2. Cut out the cereal boxes to make the farm sheds as shown. Allow to dry and glue to the large painted green cardboard.

3. Cut out the paper to form a pond shape and glue to the large painted green cardboard.

4. Create the pens for the animals with the small twigs as shown.

5. Cut out farm animals as shown.

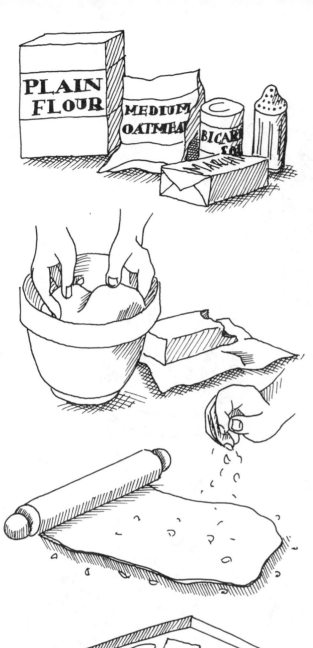

COOKING

OATCAKES

<u>YOU WILL NEED</u>

175 g (6 oz) medium oatmeal
50 g (2 oz) plain flour
40 g (1 1/2 oz) margarine
1/2 teaspoon bicarbonate of soda
1/2 teaspoon salt
boiling water to mix

Oven temperature: 200' C/400' F/Gas 6

<u>METHOD</u>

1. Mix the oatmeal, flour, bicarbonate of soda and salt in a bowl. Add the margarine, with sufficient water to give a soft binding consistency.

2. Knead lightly and roll out very thinly on a board sprinkled with a little oatmeal or flour.

3. Cut into triangles. Place on a greased baking tray and bake towards the top of the oven for about 15 minutes, or until the edges curl up and the oatcakes are crisp.

OATY BREAD

YOU WILL NEED

225 g (8 oz) wholemeal flour
25 g (1 oz) medium oatmeal
13 g (1/2 oz) margarine
13 g (1/2 oz) fresh yeast
1 teaspoonful clear honey
150 ml (1/4 pint) tepid water
Milk to glaze

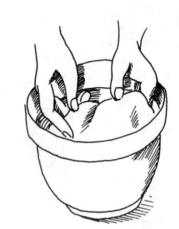

Pre heated oven temperature: 230' C/450' F/ Gas 8

METHOD

1. Place the flour in a bowl and stir in the oatmeal. Rub in the margarine.

2. Crumble the yeast into the water and stir in the honey. When dissolved, pour onto the flour and stir in with the hands. Bring together to form a dough.

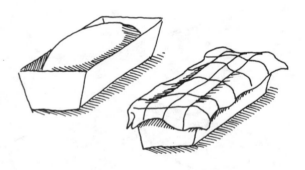

3. Turn onto a floured surface and knead until smooth. Cover and leave to rest for 10 minutes. Grease a loaf tin.

4. Then take the dough and gently shape into an oblong, three times as long as the tin. Fold into three, and with the fold underneath, place in the tin. Cover and leave to double in size in a warm place.

5. Glaze with milk and bake for 25 minutes, until golden-brown. Tip the loaf out of the tin and if it sounds hollow when tapped under-neath, it is ready.

GHANA YAM FESTIVAL

The Yam Festival, which is known as the 'To Hoot at Famine', is held during the first and second weeks of August. This is the time when the food crops on the farms begin to mature, and the fresh yams and coco yams are ready for harvest. Garden vegetables such as okra and beans are ripe, and everyone begins to forget about the hungry days of the past few months.

Even when the yams are harvested, nobody is allowed to eat them or even bring them into the markets of villages. This is because some yams have first to be ceremonially offered up to the god of the harvest and to the people's ancestors. Ancestors are honoured because it is believed they have great influence.

After the priest has carried out these rituals everyone eats a meal of new yams. The parties, with singing and dancing, can begin!

Children play games of somersault and throw-and-catch. A thick and solid coconut palm branch is cut and fixed into a hilly ground and the children somersault over it Throw-and-catch, called **Odo**, is another exciting game. A fairly thick tassel is made of palm leaves, with the mid-ribs removed. The children divide into two sides. The tassel is thrown in the air, and while it is falling back, the players stand with loops made of fibre to catch it. Whoever catches it gains a point for their group.

The yam is also an important crop in Nigeria. The Yoruba people of Nigeria are also known for their traditional festival of ancestor worship. They make offerings to the shrines of their ancestor's spirits, and dress up in elaborate costumes and masks, impersonating their spirits as they dance in the streets.

THINGS TO DO

AN AFRICAN MASK

<u>YOU WILL NEED</u>

Polyfilla, water, string or long strips of material, round bowl or balloon, raffia cut into 20 cm (8") lengths, poster paint, varnish.

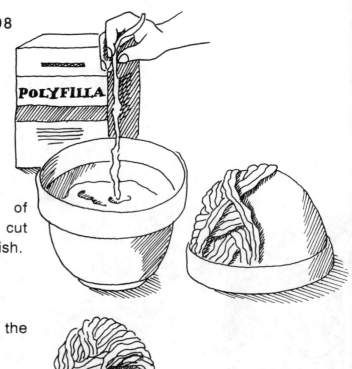

<u>METHOD</u>

1. Mix the polyfilla as instructed on the packet.

2. Dip the string or material into the polyfilla mixture, then layer it over the bowl making sure it is covered well.

3. Make holes for the eyes and mouth by pushing the string away. Make a hole towards the top and either side of the mask. This will be used to thread the string through.

4. With clean hands attach the lengths of raffia to the back of the mask to form the hair.

5. Allow to dry overnight before painting and varnishing.

DANCING PUPPET

<u>YOU WILL NEED</u>

Cardboard, scrap material.

<u>METHOD</u>

1. Draw and cut out the outline of a person. Instead of legs cut out two holes as shown.

2. Decorate the puppet. The first and second fingers go through the circle to make the puppet dance.

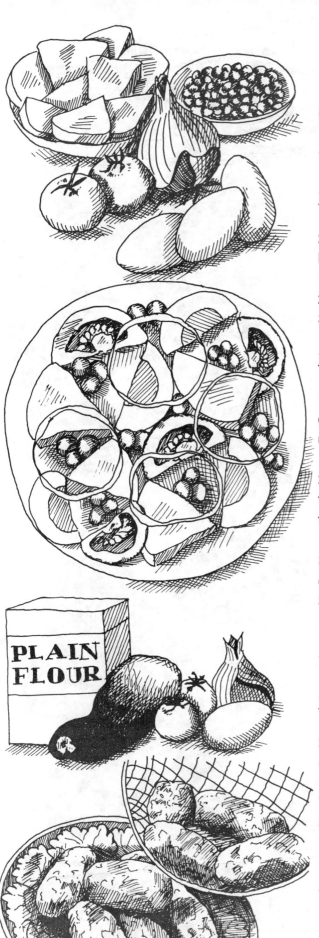

COOKING

YAM SALAD

<u>YOU WILL NEED</u>

224 g (1/2 lb) cooked yam
boiled beans or peas
1 medium sized onion
2 medium sized fresh tomatoes
3 hard boiled eggs

<u>METHOD</u>

1. Peel the yam exactly as if it were a potato cut into triangles and cook it in boiling water until tender.

2. Boil the eggs and cut them into fours. Slice the onion into rings. Cut the tomatoes into triangles.

3. Arrange the yam pieces, tomatoes, and eggs on a plate, each forming a triangle. Sprinkle with salad cream and serve cold.

YAM BALLS

<u>YOU WILL NEED</u>

200 g (7 oz) yam
45 g (1 3/4 oz) flour
15 g (3/4 oz) tomatoes
75 g (3 oz) chopped onions
Salt, pepper and oil for frying
1 egg

<u>METHOD</u>

1. Cook the yams and mash them. Blend in the egg, onion and tomatoes.

2. Roll your mixture to egg size. Fry in deep fat until brown.

AT THE SEASIDE

At first sight the sandy beaches may look empty, but on every seashore there are a whole host of different animals and plants. Some live in rocky hollows, which hold sea-water between tides. Others live buried under the sand, where it is always damp. Each animal or plant is specially adapted to living where it does. Some have suckers to hold on to rocks, others have filters to keep sand out of their breathing tubes.

TIDES

Everyone who has been to the sea has noticed how the water creeps slowly up the beach for about six hours, then for six hours slips steadily down again.

Tides are caused mainly by the gravity of the moon. Whenever the moon rises over the seas, it heaps up the water directly underneath its gravity. As the earth turns, the moon holds this bulge of water steady so that it reaches land and washes ashore as a tide. This heaping up of water also happens at the same time on the side of the earth facing away from the moon, and this is why we have two tides a day.

MOLLUSCS

Molluscs are small, soft, flabby, slow-moving animals with gills and a shell. The shell, which they have grown themselves, is made up of calcium carbonate and other minerals extracted from the sea. There are many different kinds of mollusc in the sea, such as cockles, mussels, oysters, whelks, periwinkles, and barnacles. Some are like slugs and snails that live on land. Others, called bivalves, have two hinged shells. They burrow in mud and sand. The octopus is a mollusc, although its shell is inside its body.

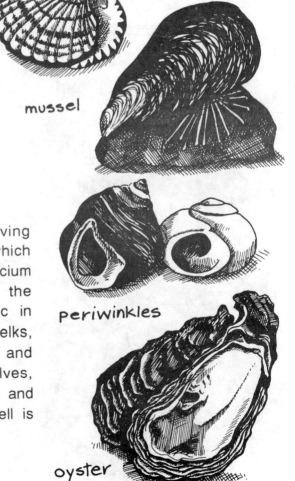

cockle

mussel

periwinkles

oyster

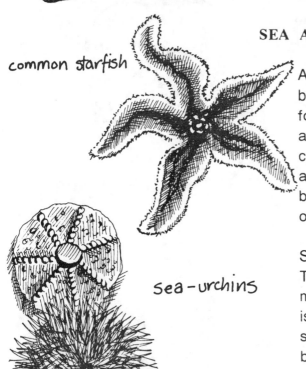

common jellyfish

lugworm

common starfish

Sea-urchins

anemone

WORMS AND JELLYFISH

There are many animals hiding on a beach. Burrowing worms are easy to find because they leave casts in the sand or mud. The lugworm is common on the sandy shores. Its soft, plump body has red feathery gills and fishermen use them for bait.

Jellyfish are among the strangest of all the sea creatures, for they are composed of a jelly-like substance which is about 98 per cent sea-water. They are umbrella-shaped, with a number of poisonous tentacles hanging down from the inside of the umbrella.

SEA ANEMONES, SEA URCHINS AND STARFISH

Anemones have the appearance of flowers but they are really living creatures, often found in shallow water attached to stones and rocks. Their bodies are short, hollow cylinders of soft flesh. They have no skeleton and their bodies have a sucker at the bottom by which the animal anchors itself. They feed on small fish that come swimming by.

Sea urchins, and starfish have spiny skins. They have chalky plates under the skin, and move on tube-like feet. The common starfish is often found on the lower shore in mud, sand and rock pools. Its colour varies from brownish-yellow to purple. It eats mussels and oysters, which it pulls open with its feet. Sea urchins are a dull green or purplish in colour. Their bristling spines protect them against small fishes and crabs. Sea urchins and starfish produce enormous quantities of eggs every summer, most of which are eaten by other marine creatures.

THE CRAB FAMILY

Crabs, prawns, lobsters, crayfish, and shrimps are all crustaceans. They are relatives of insects and spiders, and have many jointed legs. They usually have a heavy, hard outer skeleton, which makes them slow movers. They come in all shapes and sizes, and nearly all live by the sea.

The crab, like the crayfish and lobster, has feelers, eye-stalks, jaws and five other mouth-parts, five pairs of walking legs, and a shell.

The common shrimp is from two to three inches long and has ten paddle-like legs for rapid swimming, long feelers on the head, and a hump-backed, grey-green body. Prawns are like shrimps on a larger scale. One difference between the two is in the beak. A shrimp's beak is short and smooth; a prawn's is long and deeply saw-edged.

common shore crab

common shrimp

BARNACLES

It was believed at one time that barnacles were molluscs, like oysters, but they are crustaceans - relatives of the lobster and the crab. Born as free-swimming larvae, they finally cement themselves to rocks or boats by their heads. They lose their power of motion, except in the six pairs of feathery feet which project from the shell and wave food into their mouths.

barnacles

Suggested Songs: **I do like to be beside the seaside**, from **Ta-ra-ra boom-de-ay**, published by A. C. Black. **Fishing off the Jetty, Donkey Rides, Sandcastles, Fishing boats, Whispering seashells**, by Peter Canwell, published by Collins Educational.

THINGS TO DO

OBSERVING BARNACLES

<u>YOU WILL NEED</u>

A fish tank or transparent container, plastic bag, several plastic bottles, sea water.

<u>METHOD</u>

1.   Put some sea water in the empty plastic bottles. Carry the barnacles home in a plastic bag. Put the barnacles into the tank, covering them well with sea water, which they need to feed from (ordinary tap water won't do).

2. Wait and watch them unfold their long tendril-like legs, as they open up and kick microscopic food into their mouths. Change the sea water in the tank every other day, keep them out of direct sunlight, and this unusual pet will go on waving away for some time!

SAND PAINTING

<u>YOU WILL NEED</u>

Silver sand, white cardboard,   powder paint wallpaper paste (without anti-fungicide), bright adhesive tape.

<u>METHOD</u>

1. Cut the cardboard to the size you want the picture to be. Stick the adhesive tape all round the edges to make a frame for the picture.

2. Mix some sand and powder paint together. Draw a design on the card and then brush over the design with a thick layer of paste. Sprinkle the sand over the pasted area. Carefully shake off any surplus sand.

SEA SHELL SHOW CASE

<u>YOU WILL NEED</u>

Six large match boxes, a selection of sea shells, card 37 cm x 15 cm (15" x 6"), glue, tissue, blue paint.

<u>METHOD</u>

1. Remove the covers of the matchboxes. Glue the sides of the base together. Then glue these to the card. Paint the inside and outer edges of the boxes and allow to dry. The partitioning can be left in some of the boxes, depending on the sizes of the shells. Clean the shells as shown in **Sea Shell Plaque.**

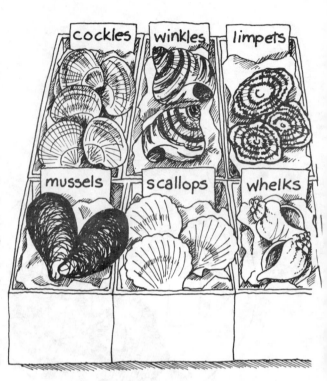

2. Line each compartment with some tissue. Sort the shells into different types and place them in the boxes.

3. Write the names of each different kind of shell on a small piece of card, and place each one in the appropriate compartment.

SEA SHELL PLAQUE

Containers such as glass bottles, empty yoghurt pots and old jars can also be covered with plaster and decorated with shells. A coat of varnish will make the shells shine and help them stay in place.

<u>YOU WILL NEED</u>

1 packet of polyfilla, paper plate, an old mixing bowl, string, an assortment of tiny shells, tweezers, round-edged knife, varnish.

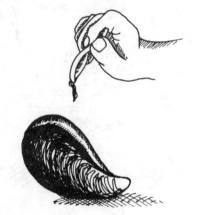

<u>METHOD</u>

1. To make sure there are no creatures inside the shells, boil them in a saucepan. Then remove any bits left inside with tweezers.

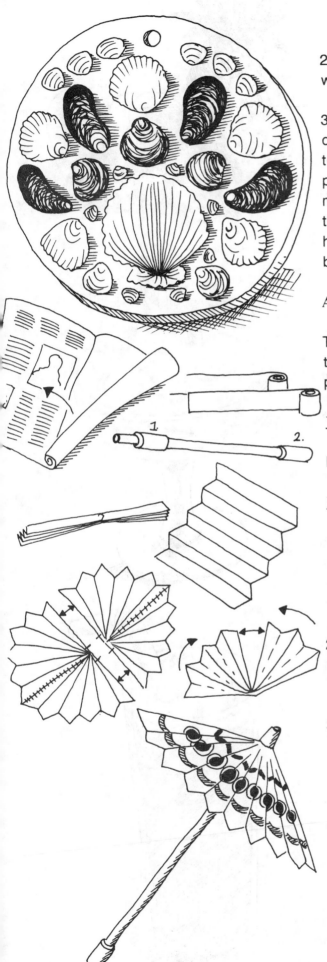

2. Wash the shells thoroughly in warm soapy water and spread them on newspaper to dry.

3. Mix the plaster in the bowl to a thick consistency. Spread the paste with the knife to about 0.5 cm (1/4") thickness all over the paper plate. Gently press the shells into the mixture to make a pattern. Pierce a hole at the top of the plate ready to thread string and hang when dry. Allow at least five days before painting all over with varnish.

A PARASOL

The word parasol means 'protection against the sun. Parasols and sunshades are very popular at seaside resorts.

YOU WILL NEED

Large Sunday paper, tape, a stapler, paint.

METHOD

1. For the handle, take six double sheets of newspaper and place them on top of each other. Roll them up and secure the roll with tape in the centre and at the ends.

2. Cut two long strips of newspaper. Roll the strips of paper at points 1 and 2 as shown. Tape in position.

3. Take two sheets of newspaper and fold into pleats. Put one staple across the centre. Then bring the two ends round until they meet and form a half-circle. Staple along the join.

4. Make the second fan in the same way. Then staple the two half-circles together, leaving a small gap at the centre as shown.

5. Push the stick through the hole in the shade. Cut a long strip of paper and roll round the top. Paint the parasol in bright colours.

COOKING

SUMMER FRUIT ICE CREAM

<u>YOU WILL NEED</u>

250 g (9 oz) fruits such as apricots, strawberries, peaches, pineapples or raspberries
50 g (2 oz) castor sugar
6 tablespoons double cream
1/2 tablespoon very hot water in a cup
1/2 teaspoon gelatine

<u>METHOD</u>

1. Use a wooden spoon to mash the fruit through a sieve. Sprinkle the gelatine into the hot water and stir briskly. The gelatine should dissolve quickly.

2. Mix the fruit, sugar and gelatine together in a bowl. When the mixture is cold, beat it well and fold in the whipped cream. Pour the mixture into an ice tray and leave in the freezer for at least three hours.

CHOCOLATE MILK SHAKE

Do an experiment with the children. Try mixing the cocoa with the milk, it won't work. Now try mixing the cocoa and sugar first - Presto! It mixes easily.

<u>YOU WILL NEED</u>

1 teaspoon of cocoa
2 teaspoons of sugar
1 cup of milk
about a tablespoon of water

<u>METHOD</u>

Mix the cocoa and sugar in a bowl. Add the water and mix thoroughly. Stir in the milk and whisk until frothy, and pour into a glass.

ACKNOWLEDGEMENTS

I wish to thank the following people.

Kate Davey, for the illustrations.

Alison Brookes, for proof reading.

Liz Orui, from the Japanese School in London, who was a great help in providing the material for the Japanese festivals, and in encouraging her class to contribute to the book.

The Nina West Nurseries, in London, who tried out and provided some of the practical ideas.

Hampstead Parochial School, for their contributions to the book

Sarah Berman, from the Yavneh Nursery in Brighton, who provided some of the background information on the Jewish Festivals.

All the friends who have helped to promote the Open-Sez-Me books.